Test Taking: Grade 3
Table of Contents

Introduction to STARS 2
Letter to Parents 4
Letter to Students 5
DOs and DON'Ts 6
STARS Record Chart 7

UNIT I: WORD ANALYSIS
Lesson 1: Analyzing Sounds in Words 8
Lesson 2: Working with Word Forms 9
Lesson 3: Choosing the Right Word 12
Practice Test 1 14

UNIT II: VOCABULARY
Lesson 1: Using Synonyms 17
Lesson 2: Finding Antonyms 19
Lesson 3: Classifying Words 21
Lesson 4: Understanding Words With More Than One Meaning 23
Lesson 5: Using Context Clues 25
Practice Test 2 29

UNIT III: SPELLING AND LANGUAGE
Lesson 1: Using Correct Spelling 35
Lesson 2: Using Correct Capitalization 37
Lesson 3: Using Correct Punctuation 39
Lesson 4: Using Correct Capitalization and Punctuation 41
Practice Test 3 44

UNIT IV: READING COMPREHENSION
Lesson 1: Reading Stories 48
Lesson 2: Choosing Titles 55
Lesson 3: Arranging Sentences in Correct Order 57
Practice Test 4 60

UNIT V: MATH PRACTICE
Lesson 1: Using Number Concepts 66
Lesson 2: Using Mixed Operations 69
Lesson 3: Using Fractions and Decimals 75
Lesson 4: Using Geometry and Measurement 77
Practice Test 5 79

UNIT VI: MATH PROBLEM SOLVING
Lesson 1: Reviewing Problem Solving Strategies 84
Practice Test 6 90

Answer Key 93
Practice Test Answer Sheet 95

Test Taking STARS
(Strategies To Achieve Raised Scores)

INTRODUCTION

Test Taking is a tool to assist your students in learning to take tests. Research shows that students who are acquainted with the scoring format of standardized tests score higher on these tests. Students also score higher when they practice and encounter the pressures of timed tests. The concepts presented for practice are typically found on standardized tests for students at the third-grade level. The scores on these activities are indicators of a student's ability to take tests, not necessarily to master the concepts used for practice. Students who practice with STARS will grow comfortable with the variety of processes needed to improve test scores.

ORGANIZATION

Each of the six units focuses on specific test taking areas in content: Word Analysis, Vocabulary, Spelling and Language, Reading Comprehension, Math Practice, and Math Problem Solving. Practice lessons introduce students to the typical formats they can expect to see. These pages identify strategy tips for improving accuracy and speed. At the bottom of each lesson, students are encouraged to evaluate their performance. Again, the goal is to improve students' ability to perform well on tests. At the end of each unit, a practice test is included. Students have the opportunity to apply the strategies they learned in the lessons and to demonstrate their abilities to successfully complete a test. Also, students can use the *STARS Record Chart* to track the number of items completed correctly on each lesson and test.

USE

STARS is designed for independent use by students who have had instruction in the specific skills covered in these workbooks. Copies of the activities can be given to individuals, pairs of students, or small groups for completion. They can also be used as a center activity.

To begin, determine the implementation which fits your students' needs and your classroom structure. The following plan suggests a format for this implementation:

1. Explain the purpose of the worksheets to your class.

2. Review the mechanics of how you want students to work with the exercises. Do you want to check the practice lessons before they begin the practice tests? Do you want to discuss the samples in each lesson?

3. Determine how the timed tests will be monitored. If students are to do the timed tests on their own, what timing instrument should they use? Do you want to administer the timed tests to the whole class or to a group that has successfully completed a series of practice lessons?

4. Introduce students to the process and to the purpose of the activities. Make copies of the **Letter to Students**. Go over the information, and review the **DOs and DON'Ts** for test taking.

5. Discuss the component of tracking progress. Give a copy of the *STARS Record Chart* to each student. Identify a place for the progress chart to be maintained, i.e., in a

folder, inside the students' notebooks, etc. (You may want to keep these progress charts to include in students' portfolios.)

6. Assure students that all of the material is for practice purposes only. It is to help them do better on tests.

7. Do a practice activity together.

ADDITIONAL NOTES

1. Time Limits. The time limits for each practice test are suggested limits. You may choose to ignore them or to set limits which you think are more appropriate for your students.

2. Parent Communication. Sign the **Letter to Parents**. Duplicate and send home with students. Encourage students to share the **Letter to Students** with their parents. Decide if you want to keep the activity pages and practice tests in portfolios for conferencing, or if you want students to take them home as they complete them.

3. Bulletin Board. Display the **DOs and DON'Ts** for test taking in your classroom for quick reference.

4. Student Evaluation. In the student evaluation section of the practice activities, encourage students to identify interferences that affect their performance on tests, i.e., conflicts with peers, lack of sleep, inadequate breakfast, etc.

5. Have fun. Reducing the pressure associated with test taking can be fun as well as meaningful for you and your students. Look forward to positive results and to improved test scores!

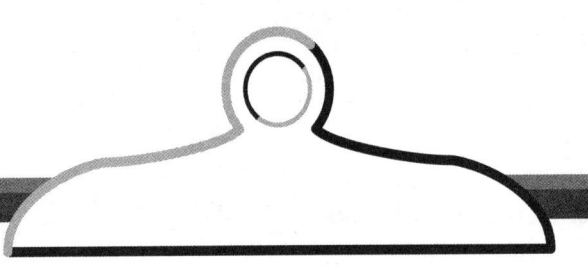

Dear Parent,

Sometime during this school year, our class will be taking mandated standardized tests. To increase your child's skills in test taking, we will be working with sample tests to give him or her the tools to perform well. Test taking can be stressful. By working together to prepare the students, we can reduce their stress level.

From time to time, I may send home lesson practice sheets. To best help your child, please consider the following suggestions:

- Provide a quiet place to work.
- Go over the directions and the sample exercises together.
- Review the Strategy Tips.
- Reassure your child that the practice sheets are not a "real" test.
- Encourage your child to do his or her best.
- Record the amount of time it takes to complete the lesson.
- Check the lesson when it is complete.
- Go over the answers and note improvements as well as problems.

Help your child maintain a positive attitude about taking a standardized test. Let your child know that each test provides an opportunity to shine. If your child expresses anxiety about taking a test or completing these lessons, help him or her understand what causes the stress. Then, talk about ways to eliminate anxiety. Above all, enjoy this time you spend with your child. He or she will feel your support, and test scores will improve as success in test taking is experienced.

Thank you for your help!

Cordially,

© Steck-Vaughn Company

Name _____ Date _____

Dear Student:

Your teacher has announced that you will be taking some tests during the school year. You're wondering how well you'll do. Many people feel anxious when they have to take a test. Suddenly they can't think, and they're sure that they have forgotten everything they ever knew. There are ways to avoid those feelings. You will be doing practice lessons and tests that will help you prepare for taking tests. In addition to the DOs and DON'Ts, you'll find strategy tips for taking specific tests on the practice pages.

As you work with practice lessons, remember the following:
- Read the directions carefully.
- Look for key words that tell exactly what you have to do.
- Read and think about the strategy tips for each lesson before beginning to work.
- Study the sample questions and the reasons given for the correct answer.
- Read each test question carefully.
- Stop working whenever you come to the word *STOP*.
- Check your answers with the teacher.
- Record your score on the special STARS chart.
- Treat the practice tests as though they are real tests.

Your practice will help you improve your test taking. Have fun as you develop new skills!

Name _____   Date _____

STARS DOs AND DON'Ts FOR TEST TAKING

DO:
- listen to or read all the directions.
- read all the samples and STRATEGY TIPS for each lesson before you begin.
- look over the entire test or section before you begin.
- stay calm, concentrate on the test, and clear your mind of things that have nothing to do with the test.
- read all the answer choices before choosing the one that you think is best.
- make sure the number you fill in on the answer sheet matches the question number on the test page.
- trust your first instinct when answering each question.
- answer the easy questions first, then go back and work on the ones you aren't sure about.
- take all the time you are allowed.

DON'T:
- look ahead to another question until you complete the one you're working on.
- spend too much time on one question.
- rush.
- worry if others finish while you are still working.
- change an answer unless you are really sure it should be changed.

DO your very best!

Student _____

STARS Record Chart

	number of questions	number right	date
Unit I: Word Analysis			
lesson 1	6	_____	_____
lesson 2	18	_____	_____
lesson 3	12	_____	_____
Practice Test 1	22	_____	_____
Unit II: Vocabulary			
lesson 1	14	_____	_____
lesson 2	12	_____	_____
lesson 3	18	_____	_____
lesson 4	12	_____	_____
lesson 5	30	_____	_____
Practice Test 2	34	_____	_____
Unit III: Spelling and Language			
lesson 1	12	_____	_____
lesson 2	10	_____	_____
lesson 3	14	_____	_____
lesson 4	12	_____	_____
Practice Test 3	24	_____	_____
Unit IV: Reading Comprehension			
lesson 1	21	_____	_____
lesson 2	5	_____	_____
lesson 3	10	_____	_____
Practice Test 4	20	_____	_____
Unit V: Math Practice			
lesson 1	14	_____	_____
lesson 2	32	_____	_____
lesson 3	10	_____	_____
lesson 4	10	_____	_____
Practice Test 5	31	_____	_____
Unit VI: Math Problem Solving			
lesson 1	12	_____	_____
Practice Test 6	14	_____	_____

© Steck-Vaughn Company

Test Taking 3, SV 6973-8

Name _____ Date _____

UNIT I: WORD ANALYSIS

Lesson 1: Analyzing sounds in words

DIRECTIONS ▶ Darken the circle for the word that <u>does not</u> have the same sound as the underlined part of the word.

STRATEGY TIPS

1. Reread the directions. Remember that you are looking for the word that <u>does not</u> have the same sound as the underlined word.
2. Say each word to yourself. Decide which word <u>does not</u> sound like the other three, even if they have the same letters.

Sample:

k<u>ee</u>p

Ⓐ leap
Ⓑ deed
Ⓒ head
Ⓓ knee

ANSWER

The correct answer is *C. head.* *Leap, deed,* and *knee* all have the same long *e* sound as *keep. Head* does not have the same sound.

NOW TRY THESE

1. <u>ch</u>oose
   Ⓐ teach
   Ⓑ bench
   Ⓒ cheap
   Ⓓ ache

2. n<u>i</u>ght
   Ⓔ winter
   Ⓕ cry
   Ⓖ dye
   Ⓗ life

3. <u>th</u>ing
   Ⓐ think
   Ⓑ thirst
   Ⓒ there
   Ⓓ thief

4. h<u>ou</u>se
   Ⓔ out
   Ⓕ could
   Ⓖ crown
   Ⓗ foul

5. b<u>e</u>nd
   Ⓐ west
   Ⓑ egg
   Ⓒ net
   Ⓓ here

6. w<u>a</u>ll
   Ⓔ bald
   Ⓕ awe
   Ⓖ sack
   Ⓗ watch

STOP

Your time: _____

Number right: _____

Name _____   Date _____

Lesson 2: Working with word forms
Part one

DIRECTIONS ▶ Darken the circle that shows the prefix for each word.

STRATEGY TIPS

1. Look for a smaller word within the given word that can stand alone.
2. The prefix is in front of this word and changes the meaning of the smaller word.

Sample:

    remove
    Ⓐ move
    Ⓑ re
    Ⓒ rem
    Ⓓ ove

ANSWER

The correct answer is *B. re*. *Move* is a word that can stand by itself. *Re* is the prefix which is added to the word *move*.

NOW TRY THESE

1. inland
   Ⓐ and
   Ⓑ land
   Ⓒ in
   Ⓓ an

2. repeat
   Ⓔ peat
   Ⓕ rep
   Ⓖ eat
   Ⓗ re

3. discount
   Ⓐ dis
   Ⓑ disc
   Ⓒ count
   Ⓓ ount

4. preview
   Ⓔ view
   Ⓕ rev
   Ⓖ pre
   Ⓗ review

5. unbelievable
   Ⓐ able
   Ⓑ un
   Ⓒ believe
   Ⓓ belie

6. misprint
   Ⓔ print
   Ⓕ misp
   Ⓖ sprint
   Ⓗ mis

STOP

Your time: _____

Number right: _____

On this lesson I did _____ because _____

_____.

Name _____   Date _____

Lesson 2: Working with word forms
Part two

DIRECTIONS ▶ Darken the circle for the word that best completes each sentence.

STRATEGY TIPS
1. Read each sentence.
2. Read each word choice to find the one that makes sense.

Sample:
We _____ tetherball at recess yesterday.

- Ⓐ playing
- Ⓑ plays
- Ⓒ played
- Ⓓ play

ANSWER

The correct answer is *C. played*. *Playing*, *plays*, and *play* do not fit in this sentence.

NOW TRY THESE

7. The teacher was _____ to the class.
   - Ⓐ talk
   - Ⓑ talked
   - Ⓒ talking
   - Ⓓ talks

8. Use a broom to _____ the floor.
   - Ⓔ sweeping
   - Ⓕ sweep
   - Ⓖ swept
   - Ⓗ sweeps

9. Thu is _____ her first cake.
   - Ⓐ baking
   - Ⓑ bakes
   - Ⓒ bake
   - Ⓓ baked

10. The queen _____ a crown on her head.
    - Ⓔ wear
    - Ⓕ wearing
    - Ⓖ wears
    - Ⓗ worn

GO ON TO NEXT PAGE ▶

Name _____   Date _____

Unit 1, lesson 2, part 2, page 2

11. The wind _____ through the trees.
    - Ⓐ blowing
    - Ⓑ blown
    - Ⓒ blow
    - Ⓓ blows

12. We _____ a new digital clock.
    - Ⓔ bought
    - Ⓕ buys
    - Ⓖ buying
    - Ⓗ buy

13. Do you want to _____ a glass of water?
    - Ⓐ drank
    - Ⓑ drinking
    - Ⓒ drunk
    - Ⓓ drink

14. Food is _____ on a platter.
    - Ⓔ serve
    - Ⓕ serving
    - Ⓖ served
    - Ⓗ server

15. Beans _____ in our garden.
    - Ⓐ grown
    - Ⓑ grows
    - Ⓒ growing
    - Ⓓ grow

16. They went _____ on their new bikes.
    - Ⓔ rode
    - Ⓕ rides
    - Ⓖ ride
    - Ⓗ riding

17. The children _____ at the funny clown.
    - Ⓐ laughed
    - Ⓑ laughing
    - Ⓒ laughs
    - Ⓓ laughter

18. We all felt sad when we had to _____ .
    - Ⓔ leaving
    - Ⓕ left
    - Ⓖ leave
    - Ⓗ leaves

STOP

Your time: _____

Number right: _____

On this lesson I did _____ because _____

_____ .

© Steck-Vaughn Company   Test Taking 3, SV 6973-8

Name _____   Date _____

Lesson 3: Choosing the right word

DIRECTIONS ▶ Darken the circle for the word that finishes each sentence correctly.

STRATEGY TIPS

1. Say each word to yourself before choosing the answer.
2. Many words look alike, so look carefully to make sure you choose the word that makes sense in the sentence.

Sample:
We can catch fish in _____.

Ⓐ nests
Ⓑ nots
Ⓒ nuts
Ⓓ nets

ANSWER

The correct answer is *D. nets*. *Nests*, *nots*, and *nuts* look almost like *nets*, but they do not make sense in the sentence.

NOW TRY THESE

1. There are flowers _____.
   Ⓐ everybody
   Ⓑ everyone
   Ⓒ everywhere
   Ⓓ everything

2. Lumber can be cut into _____.
   Ⓔ boards
   Ⓕ breads
   Ⓖ beards
   Ⓗ bands

3. _____ is another word for seashore.
   Ⓐ Leach
   Ⓑ Reach
   Ⓒ Teach
   Ⓓ Beach

4. Cars travel on _____.
   Ⓔ lank
   Ⓕ lane
   Ⓖ land
   Ⓗ lamb

5. That candy bar will _____ one dollar.
   Ⓐ cost
   Ⓑ lost
   Ⓒ costing
   Ⓓ most

6. They built a cabin made of _____.
   Ⓔ hood
   Ⓕ wood
   Ⓖ wool
   Ⓗ wooden

GO ON TO NEXT PAGE

Name _____   Date _____

Unit 1, lesson 3, page 2

7. Do you _____ the fire burning?

   Ⓐ small
   Ⓑ smile
   Ⓒ smell
   Ⓓ sell

8. We went to a _____ concert in the park.

   Ⓔ bend
   Ⓕ band
   Ⓖ bind
   Ⓗ brand

9. I think that _____ likes ice cream.

   Ⓐ everything
   Ⓑ anything
   Ⓒ everyone
   Ⓓ anywhere

10. Jody found a _____ dog near her home.

    Ⓔ stray
    Ⓕ strand
    Ⓖ star
    Ⓗ story

11. Chan _____ at his friend's house last night.

    Ⓐ slip
    Ⓑ swept
    Ⓒ slapped
    Ⓓ slept

12. _____ is another word for cry.

    Ⓔ Wipe
    Ⓕ Weep
    Ⓖ Sleep
    Ⓗ Weak

Your time: _____

Number right: _____

On this lesson I did _____ because _____.

I think it would help me to _____

_____.

Name _____   Date _____

PRACTICE TEST 1

Practice Test Answer Sheet, p. 95

Part 1

Directions: For questions 1–4, find the word that does not have the same sound as the underlined part of the word. Fill in the space on the answer sheet for the best answer.

       Sample: girl
                      A page   C going
                      B give   D bag

Answer: The correct answer is *A. page*. The letter *g* in the other words sounds like the *g* in *girl*.

---

1. **wink**
 A mind   C sing
 B ring   D pink

2. **scare**
 E school   G score
 F scissors   H scone

3. **lost**
 A toss   C cost
 B moss   D most

4. **star**
 E stare   G cart
 F large   H barn

Directions: For questions 5–8, find the letter that shows the prefix for each word. Fill in the space on the answer sheet for the best answer.

       Sample: rewind
                      A wind   C nd
                      B re   D win

Answer: The correct answer is *B. re*. This is the prefix added to the word *wind*.

---

5. **indoor**
 A in   C door
 B or   D do

6. **discover**
 E er   G cove
 F dis   H er

7. **replace**
 A place   C re
 B pl   D rep

8. **unlike**
 E lik   G un
 F like   H ke

GO ON TO NEXT PAGE

© Steck-Vaughn Company   14   Test Taking 3, SV 6973-8

Name _____   Date _____

Part 2

Directions: For questions 9–16, choose the word that finishes each sentence correctly. Fill in the space on the answer sheet for the best answer.

Sample: Jason enjoys all outdoor _____.

A sport C sporting
B sported D sports

Answer: The correct answer is *D. sports*. The other words do not fit in this sentence.

---

9. We go _____ in the summer.

   A camping C camp
   B camped D camper

10. Jessica was _____ to a birthday party.

    E invite G invites
    F inviting H invited

11. Joe used a net to _____ the fish out of the tank.

    A takes C take
    B taking D took

12. Zalmon was _____ his glass with water.

    E filling G fills
    F fill H filled

13. Mia accidentally _____ the handle on the cup.

    A broke C broken
    B brake D braking

14. Fred _____ a picture in art class.

    E drawn G drew
    F drawing H draw

15. He _____ the envelope before he mailed it.

    A addressed C address
    B addressing D addresses

16. Please _____ the story to me.

    E explained G explaining
    F explains H explain

GO ON TO NEXT PAGE

Name _____   Date _____

Part 3

Directions: For questions 17–22, find the word that best completes each sentence. Fill in the space on the answer sheet for the best answer.

Sample: Tie a knot in the _____ .

      A   rip   C   rope
      B   ripe   D   rob

Answer: The correct answer is *B. rope. Rip*, *ripe*, and *rob* look almost like *rope*, but they do not make sense in the sentence.

---

17. Take a _____ after lunch.

    A   best   C   nest
    B   rest   D   west

18. Please _____ me a pencil.

    E   wind   G   lend
    F   land   H   wand

19. What will you _____ to the picnic?

    A   brag   C   brim
    B   brink   D   bring

20. Don't _____ away from the group.

    E   wander   G   wonder
    F   water   H   winter

21. We watched a funny program _____ night.

    A   lost   C   list
    B   lash   D   last

22. I will _____ this letter.

    E   mail   G   mall
    F   rail   H   make

STOP

Suggested Time Limit: 22 minutes   Your time: _____

Check your work if you have time. Wait for instructions from your teacher.

Name _____ Date _____

UNIT II: VOCABULARY

Lesson 1: Using synonyms

DIRECTIONS ▶ Darken the circle for the choice that has the same or almost the same meaning as the underlined word.

STRATEGY TIPS

1. Think about what the underlined word means.
2. Try saying each choice in place of the underlined word.
3. Use the underlined word in phrases of your own.

Sample:

    seal the envelope

    Ⓐ close
    Ⓑ mail
    Ⓒ open
    Ⓓ receive

ANSWER

The correct answer is A. *close*. *Seal* means *close*. Although *mail*, *open*, and *receive* make sense in the phrase, only *close* means almost the same as *seal*.

NOW TRY THESE

1. chant a tune
    Ⓐ speak
    Ⓑ play
    Ⓒ remember
    Ⓓ sing

2. total eclipse
    Ⓔ add
    Ⓕ destroy
    Ⓖ complete
    Ⓗ sing

3. spiteful person
    Ⓐ mean
    Ⓑ kind
    Ⓒ happy
    Ⓓ good

4. damp clothes
    Ⓔ dirty
    Ⓕ wet
    Ⓖ clean
    Ⓗ dry

5. follow directions
    Ⓐ ignore
    Ⓑ obey
    Ⓒ think about
    Ⓓ misunderstand

6. roam down a path
    Ⓔ skip
    Ⓕ wander
    Ⓖ fall
    Ⓗ swing

GO ON TO NEXT PAGE

Name _____   Date _____

Unit 2, lesson 1, page 2

7. a <u>blanket</u> of snow
   - Ⓐ mountain
   - Ⓑ cover
   - Ⓒ scene
   - Ⓓ block

8. an <u>inquisitive</u> child
   - Ⓔ happy
   - Ⓕ silly
   - Ⓖ funny
   - Ⓗ curious

9. <u>precise</u> instructions
   - Ⓐ easy
   - Ⓑ printed
   - Ⓒ long
   - Ⓓ exact

10. <u>disturb</u> others
    - Ⓔ bother
    - Ⓕ please
    - Ⓖ practice
    - Ⓗ reward

11. <u>replace</u> books
    - Ⓐ recover
    - Ⓑ return
    - Ⓒ reread
    - Ⓓ review

12. <u>demand</u> an answer
    - Ⓔ write
    - Ⓕ recite
    - Ⓖ insist on
    - Ⓗ correct

13. <u>important</u> events
    - Ⓐ careful
    - Ⓑ special
    - Ⓒ strange
    - Ⓓ busy

14. <u>appear</u> happy
    - Ⓔ grow
    - Ⓕ stay
    - Ⓖ look
    - Ⓗ feel

STOP

Your time: _____

Number right: _____

On this lesson I did _____ because _____.

I think it would help me to _____

_____.

Name _____   Date _____

Lesson 2: Finding antonyms

DIRECTIONS ▶ Darken the circle for the word that means the opposite of the underlined word.

STRATEGY TIPS

1. Say each word.
2. Compare it to the underlined word.
3. Which word's meaning is the opposite of the underlined word?

Sample:

the strong boy

Ⓐ small
Ⓑ silly
Ⓒ weak
Ⓓ worried

ANSWER

The correct answer is *C. weak*. *Strong* means *powerful*. *Small, silly,* and *worried* make sense in the phrase, but they don't have the opposite meaning of *strong*. The opposite of *strong* is very little power, or *weak*.

NOW TRY THESE

1. a tall tree

   Ⓐ full
   Ⓑ short
   Ⓒ wide
   Ⓓ round

2. the young woman

   Ⓔ pretty
   Ⓕ thin
   Ⓖ small
   Ⓗ old

3. after dinner

   Ⓐ sooner
   Ⓑ later
   Ⓒ before
   Ⓓ earlier

4. quick as a wink

   Ⓔ slow
   Ⓕ still
   Ⓖ cross
   Ⓗ wise

5. cheap toys

   Ⓐ idle
   Ⓑ cheerful
   Ⓒ deep
   Ⓓ expensive

6. polite children

   Ⓔ careless
   Ⓕ rude
   Ⓖ happy
   Ⓗ angry

GO ON TO NEXT PAGE ▶

© Steck-Vaughn Company   Test Taking 3, SV 6973-8

Name _____   Date _____

Unit 2, lesson 2, page 2

7. <u>absent</u> because of illness
   - Ⓐ away
   - Ⓑ returned
   - Ⓒ present
   - Ⓓ gone

8. in a <u>southern</u> direction
   - Ⓔ west
   - Ⓕ warm
   - Ⓖ cold
   - Ⓗ northern

9. a <u>healthy</u> man
   - Ⓐ grumpy
   - Ⓑ sick
   - Ⓒ sing
   - Ⓓ pleased

10. a <u>rich</u> person
    - Ⓔ gold
    - Ⓕ strong
    - Ⓖ poor
    - Ⓗ loud

11. <u>lead</u> the band
    - Ⓐ play
    - Ⓑ chase
    - Ⓒ run
    - Ⓓ follow

12. turn <u>right</u>
    - Ⓔ better
    - Ⓕ good
    - Ⓖ left
    - Ⓗ like

Your time: _____

Number right: _____

On this lesson I did _____ because _____

_____.

I think it would help me to _____

_____

_____.

Name _____   Date _____

Lesson 3: Classifying words

DIRECTIONS ▶ Darken the circle for the letter of the word that <u>does not</u> belong with the other words in the group.

STRATEGY TIPS

1. Read each group of words below.
2. Think about why three of the words belong in the same group.
3. Then find the word that does not belong with them.

Sample:

- Ⓐ peanuts
- Ⓑ walnuts
- Ⓒ almonds
- Ⓓ apples

ANSWER

The correct answer is *D. apples*. Although all the words stand for things to eat, three of the words are about a certain kind of food—nuts. *Apples* are fruit, so this word doesn't belong with a group of words about nuts.

NOW TRY THESE

1. Ⓐ screwdriver Ⓒ saw
   Ⓑ table   Ⓓ hammer

2. Ⓔ orange   Ⓖ milk
   Ⓕ water   Ⓗ coffee

3. Ⓐ cup   Ⓒ oven
   Ⓑ plate   Ⓓ dish

4. Ⓔ blue   Ⓖ grass
   Ⓕ green   Ⓗ black

5. Ⓐ spoon   Ⓒ chair
   Ⓑ bed   Ⓓ couch

6. Ⓔ dog   Ⓖ cat
   Ⓕ robin   Ⓗ pig

7. Ⓐ people   Ⓒ hand
   Ⓑ arm   Ⓓ foot

8. Ⓔ eye   Ⓖ knee
   Ⓕ ear   Ⓗ nose

9. Ⓐ April   Ⓒ Friday
   Ⓑ Monday   Ⓓ Thursday

10. Ⓔ inside   Ⓖ always
    Ⓕ outside Ⓗ under

GO ON TO NEXT PAGE ▶

Name _____ Date _____

Unit 2, lesson 3, page 2

11. Ⓐ kitten   Ⓒ calf
    Ⓑ puppy   Ⓓ horse

12. Ⓔ street   Ⓖ dirt
    Ⓕ road   Ⓗ path

13. Ⓐ cherry   Ⓒ pear
    Ⓑ steak   Ⓓ peach

14. Ⓔ chocolate Ⓖ ice cream
    Ⓕ vanilla   Ⓗ strawberry

15. Ⓐ eight   Ⓒ number
    Ⓑ fifty   Ⓓ twenty-three

16. Ⓔ two dollars   Ⓖ one quarter
    Ⓕ fifteen cents Ⓗ money

17. Ⓐ sleep   Ⓒ jump
    Ⓑ action   Ⓓ read

18. Ⓔ petal   Ⓖ rose
    Ⓕ tulip   Ⓗ lily

STOP

Your time: _____

Number right: _____

On this lesson I did _____ because _____
_____.

I think it would help me to _____
_____
_____.

Name_____ Date _____

Lesson 4: Understanding words with more than one meaning

DIRECTIONS ▶ Darken the circle for the word that has both underlined meanings.

STRATEGY TIPS

1. The meanings of many words usually depend on the context in which they are used.
2. Read the definitions of the underlined words carefully.
3. Think of the one word that has both underlined meanings.

Sample:

<u>you have one when you sit</u>
<u>part of a race</u>

- Ⓐ tie
- Ⓑ lap
- Ⓒ flag
- Ⓓ tape

ANSWER

The correct answer is *B. lap*. When we sit, we form a *lap*. A complete turn on a racetrack is called a *lap*.

NOW TRY THESE

1. <u>soccer</u>
   <u>wild animals that are hunted</u>
   - Ⓐ toy
   - Ⓑ jungle
   - Ⓒ game
   - Ⓓ sport

2. <u>used to style hair</u>
   <u>on top of a rooster's head</u>
   - Ⓔ mousse
   - Ⓕ comb
   - Ⓖ brush
   - Ⓗ feather

3. <u>center of a storm</u>
   <u>what we use to see with</u>
   - Ⓐ rain
   - Ⓑ thunder
   - Ⓒ glass
   - Ⓓ eye

4. <u>a kind of snake</u>
   <u>a baby's toy</u>
   - Ⓔ cobra
   - Ⓕ rattle
   - Ⓖ block
   - Ⓗ garter

5. <u>something to sleep in</u>
   <u>a place to grow flowers</u>
   - Ⓐ bed
   - Ⓑ soil
   - Ⓒ cot
   - Ⓓ bag

6. <u>wear it on a finger</u>
   <u>the sound of a bell</u>
   - Ⓔ ring
   - Ⓕ buzz
   - Ⓖ mitten
   - Ⓗ chime

GO ON TO NEXT PAGE ▶

Name_____ Date _____

Unit 2, lesson 4, page 2

7. tell to leave a job
   start with matches
   - Ⓐ fire
   - Ⓑ scratch
   - Ⓒ hire
   - Ⓓ smoke

8. grows on a corn stalk
   what we hear with
   - Ⓔ cob
   - Ⓕ kernel
   - Ⓖ ear
   - Ⓗ drum

9. a tool for cutting wood
   observed something
   - Ⓐ hammer
   - Ⓑ knew
   - Ⓒ told
   - Ⓓ saw

10. it cools the air
    someone who roots for a team
    - Ⓔ wind
    - Ⓕ fan
    - Ⓖ coach
    - Ⓗ rain

11. it's found in a shoe
    you have one in your mouth
    - Ⓐ lace
    - Ⓑ tooth
    - Ⓒ tongue
    - Ⓓ heel

12. used to mail a letter
    put your foot down hard
    - Ⓔ walk
    - Ⓕ dance
    - Ⓖ address
    - Ⓗ stamp

Your time: _____

Number right: _____

On this lesson I did _____ because _____.

I think it would help me to _____.

Name _____   Date _____

Lesson 5: Using context clues

DIRECTIONS ▶ Darken the circle for the word that best fits each sentence in the paragraphs below.

STRATEGY TIPS

1. Read all the words in each paragraph.
2. Read the choices.
3. Use the context, all the words in the sentences, to help you decide which word makes sense in each sentence.

Sample:

We get lumber from ___(S1)___ that are cut down in the woods. Lumber is used to make __(S2)__ and other useful items.

S1 Ⓐ twigs   Ⓒ trees
    Ⓑ roots   Ⓓ flowers

S2 Ⓔ furniture   Ⓖ clothes
    Ⓕ branches   Ⓗ flags

ANSWER

The correct answer for S1 is *C. trees*. The clue words are *cut down in the woods*. We don't usually go to the woods to cut down *twigs, roots,* or *flowers*. The correct answer for S2 is *E. furniture*. Do you know why?

NOW TRY THESE

Good basketball players practice __(1)__ the ball every day. Practicing is the way they get to be __(2)__.

1. Ⓐ chasing   Ⓒ hunting
   Ⓑ shooting   Ⓓ jumping

2. Ⓔ singers   Ⓖ dancers
   Ⓕ teachers   Ⓗ winners

Squirrels __(3)__ from tree to tree searching for food. They __(4)__ the food in the ground for the winter.

3. Ⓐ dart   Ⓒ sleep
   Ⓑ dig   Ⓓ trip

4. Ⓔ chew   Ⓖ cut
   Ⓕ lost   Ⓗ bury

GO ON TO NEXT PAGE

Name _____   Date _____

Unit 2, lesson 5, page 2

We __(5)__ mothers on the second Sunday in May. Mother's Day is a __(6)__ holiday that is observed in our country.

5. Ⓐ teach   Ⓒ honor
   Ⓑ bring   Ⓓ see

6. Ⓔ sad   Ⓖ silly
   Ⓕ national Ⓗ colorful

Did you read the weather __(7)__ for today? I hope it snows so we can go __(8)__ tomorrow.

7. Ⓐ man   Ⓒ book
   Ⓑ series   Ⓓ forecast

8. Ⓔ swimming Ⓖ sailing
   Ⓕ sledding Ⓗ hiking

Sounds can __(9)__ through air and water. __(10)__ happen when a sound bounces back through air because it hits a solid wall.

9. Ⓐ shiver   Ⓒ travel
   Ⓑ climb   Ⓓ drip

10. Ⓔ Smiles Ⓖ Stories
    Ⓕ Movies Ⓗ Echoes

People are __(11)__ about the amount of water we waste. They are worried about the __(12)__ of water for the future.

11. Ⓐ concerned Ⓒ happy
    Ⓑ carefree Ⓓ helpful

12. Ⓔ color   Ⓖ taste
    Ⓕ supply   Ⓗ weight

Many people enjoy going to __(13)__ movies. The scarier the __(14)__, the better they like it.

13. Ⓐ silly   Ⓒ silent
    Ⓑ horror   Ⓓ cowboy

14. Ⓔ meal   Ⓖ ride
    Ⓕ clothes Ⓗ film

Libraries have many __(15)__ . Libraries are good places to sit and __(16)__ .

15. Ⓐ toys   Ⓒ food
    Ⓑ books   Ⓓ people

16. Ⓔ talk   Ⓖ read
    Ⓕ eat   Ⓗ play

GO ON TO NEXT PAGE

Name _____   Date_____

Unit 2, lesson 5, page 3

People go places in many different ways. Some people like to fly on a __(17)__ . Others like to __(18)__ by boat. Many people use a car to get from place to place.

17. Ⓐ bird   Ⓒ plane
    Ⓑ wind   Ⓓ train

18. Ⓔ travel   Ⓖ trade
    Ⓕ sink   Ⓗ fish

There are billions of stars surrounding the Earth. If you look in the sky on a clear night, you can see constellations. These are groups of __(19)__ that form a shape. People have given a __(20)__ to each one.

19. Ⓐ planets   Ⓒ people
    Ⓑ stars   Ⓓ ships

20. Ⓔ person   Ⓖ name
    Ⓕ rocket   Ⓗ planet

A legend is an old story. It is a __(21)__ that has been around for a long time. People have passed these stories from generation to generation. Some of them have been __(22)__ so we can remember them and read them.

21. Ⓐ person   Ⓒ lie
    Ⓑ animal   Ⓓ tale

22. Ⓔ written   Ⓖ called
    Ⓕ eaten   Ⓗ hurt

Dentists help take care of your __(23)__. A dentist will clean them and fill any cavities. Most dentists will tell you to __(24)__ twice every day, so you will have a healthy and beautiful smile.

23. Ⓐ feet   Ⓒ pets
    Ⓑ teeth   Ⓓ friends

24. Ⓔ brush   Ⓖ sleep
    Ⓕ run   Ⓗ laugh

GO ON TO NEXT PAGE

© Steck-Vaughn Company   Test Taking 3, SV 6973-8

Name _____   Date _____

Unit 2, lesson 5, page 4

Do you have a hobby? There are many kinds of hobbies. Some people like to __(25)__ a sport as a hobby. Other people like to collect things. Your hobby can be anything that you __(26)__ doing.

25. Ⓐ play   Ⓒ run
    Ⓑ throw   Ⓓ own

26. Ⓔ eat   Ⓖ remember
    Ⓕ enjoy   Ⓗ dislike

There are many things to watch for on a road trip. As you ride in the car, look carefully at the __(27)__ . They will offer directions and warnings. They __(28)__ people when they are driving.

27. Ⓐ cars   Ⓒ signs
    Ⓑ food   Ⓓ road

28. Ⓔ eat   Ⓖ find
    Ⓕ have   Ⓗ help

The post office is an interesting place. People who __(29)__ at the post office keep track of many letters. They also send packages. The post office is in charge of the __(30)__ .

29. Ⓐ play   Ⓒ work
    Ⓑ eat   Ⓓ run

30. Ⓔ mail   Ⓖ jobs
    Ⓕ boys   Ⓗ help

STOP

Your time: _____

Number right: _____

On this lesson I did _____ because _____

_____.

I think it would help me to _____

_____.

Name _____ Date _____

Practice Test 2

Practice Test Answer Sheet, p. 95

Reminder: Be sure to read the directions before you begin each part.

Part 1

Directions: For questions 1–6, choose the word that has the same or almost the same meaning as the underlined word. Record your answer on the answer sheet.

Sample: a <u>beautiful</u> picture

   A lovely   C ugly
   B large   D terrible

Answer: The correct answer is *A. lovely*. Something *beautiful* is pleasing to see. Things that are *ugly* or *terrible* are not usually pleasing to see. A *large* picture could or could not be pleasing to see.

---

1. <u>close</u> the door
   A open   C shut
   B touch   D see

2. move <u>rapidly</u>
   E stiffly   G slowly
   F swiftly   H freely

3. a <u>huge</u> animal
   A strong   C rare
   B tiny   D giant

4. <u>purchase</u> a book
   E buy   G read
   F write   H borrow

5. make <u>mistakes</u>
   A tests   C errors
   B examples   D corrections

6. go on a <u>journey</u>
   E hike   G trip
   F mile   H train

GO ON TO NEXT PAGE

Name _____ Date _____

Part 2

Directions: For questions 7–12, choose the word that means the opposite of the underlined word. Record your answer on the answer sheet.

Sample: <u>deep</u> water

    A well   C wide
    B shallow   D cold

Answer: The correct answer is *B. shallow*. *Shallow* means not deep. *Well*, *wide*, and *cold* make sense in the phrase, but they do not have the opposite meaning of *deep*.

---

7. a <u>straight</u> line
    A sharp   C crooked
    B dotted   D short

8. <u>careful</u> work
    E good   G hard
    F interesting   H careless

9. play <u>outside</u>
    A quietly   C alone
    B inside   D inward

10. a <u>sharp</u> point
    E fine   G dull
    F sticky   H long

11. the <u>strong</u> man
    A tall   C wise
    B strange   D weak

12. a <u>noisy</u> group
    E loud   G happy
    F quiet   H silly

GO ON TO NEXT PAGE

Name _____   Date _____

Part 3

Directions: For questions 13–18, choose the word that <u>does not</u> belong with the other words in the group. Record your answer on the answer sheet.

Sample: A   corn   C   peas
             B   bread   D   tomatoes

Answer: The correct answer is *B. bread*. The other words are about food from plants. *Bread* is food we make.

---

13. A   kite   C   bat
     B   ball   D   house

14. E   sun   G   ocean
     F   moon   H   stars

15. A   street   C   spring
     B   summer   D   winter

16. E   speak   G   word
     F   say   H   tell

17. A   island   C   river
     B   brook   D   lake

18. E   stories   G   pencils
     F   poems   H   songs

GO ON TO NEXT PAGE

Name_____ Date_____

Part 4

Directions: For questions 19–26, choose the word with both underlined meanings. Record your answer on the answer sheet.

Sample: a written message
read in music

A tune   C note
B bar   D song

Answer: The correct answer is *C. note*. A written message is called a note. To read music, you read the notes.

---

19. a measurement
    a place to play

    A inch   C foot
    B yard   D park

20. a kind of porch
    a pack of cards

    E patio   G set
    F veranda H deck

21. teach a pet tricks
    travels on rails

    A heel   C plane
    B train   D walk

22. country celebration
    good weather

    E party   G sunny
    F festival H fair

23. sharp part of a knife
    one piece of grass

    A blade   C point
    B leaf   D handle

24. record songs
    fasten with a sticky strip

    E tie   G rope
    F sing   H tape

25. fill a suitcase
    group of wild animals

    A herd   C pack
    B trip   D lift

26. layer of paint
    wear this to keep warm

    E brush   G scarf
    F coat   H color

GO ON TO NEXT PAGE

© Steck-Vaughn Company   32   Test Taking 3, SV 6973-8

Name_____ Date_____

Part 5

Directions: For questions 27–34, choose the letter of the word that best fits the sentences in the paragraphs below. Record your answer on the answer sheet.

Sample: Long ago, Native Americans lived in houses made of animal __(S1)__. The houses were called *tepees*. The women in the tribe made dyes and __(S2)__ pictures of the sun, moon, and stars on their tepees.

S1   **A** plastic   **C** straw
      B bricks   **D** skins

S2   **E** trained   **G** trimmed
      F painted   **H** pasted

Answer: The correct answer for S1 is *D. skins*. The other materials don't come from animals. The correct answer for S2 is *F. painted*. The clue word in the sentence is *dyes*. Dyes are not *trained, trimmed,* or *pasted*.

During the War of 1812, there were many harsh __(27)__ fought. Francis Scott Key, a young poet, watched one of the fights. When it was over, he wrote a __(28)__ called the *Star Spangled Banner*.

27. **A** storms   **C** battles
     B arguments   **D** lessons

28. **E** letter   **G** movie
     F book   **H** poem

Classrooms are a kind of community. People in the class work together so everyone can learn. Each student has __(29)__ to do. Often one student is __(30)__ as class president.

29. **A** crops   **C** jobs
     B trips   **D** ideas

30. **E** chosen   **G** tied
     F changed   **H** driven

GO ON TO NEXT PAGE

Name _____ Date _____

Weather forecasters use many __(31)__ to tell us about the weather. They can tell how hot or cold it will be. They can tell in which __(32)__ the wind is blowing.

A sea peach is not a fruit. It is an animal that lives deep in the __(33)__ of the ocean. It has two holes in its body. One takes in food and water. The other __(34)__ water out.

31. A tricks   C games
    B instruments D tiles

32. E house   G direction
    F window   H kitchen

33. A fish   C surface
    B bottom   D foam

34. E squirts   G sings
    F dries   H fans

Suggested Time Limit: 28 minutes   Your time: _____

Check your work if you have time. Wait for instructions from your teacher.

Name _____ Date _____

UNIT III: SPELLING AND LANGUAGE

Lesson 1: Using correct spelling

DIRECTIONS ▸ Darken the circle for the correctly spelled word that makes sense in each sentence.

STRATEGY TIPS
1. Read the sentence.
2. Think about the word that makes sense in the blank space, then look at the word choices.
3. Choose the word that looks like one you have probably seen.

Sample:
Park the car in the _____.
- Ⓐ garge
- Ⓒ grage
- Ⓑ graege
- Ⓓ garage

ANSWER
The correct answer is *D. garage*. The other choices may have the same letters, but they are not words.

NOW TRY THESE

1. Ellen ____ a new dress for the party.
   - Ⓐ baught
   - Ⓒ bort
   - Ⓑ bawt
   - Ⓓ bought

2. The ____ liked the show.
   - Ⓔ ordience
   - Ⓖ audience
   - Ⓕ audients
   - Ⓗ audent

3. My ____ planted a rock garden.
   - Ⓐ nabor
   - Ⓒ neghbor
   - Ⓑ neighbor
   - Ⓓ nieghbor

4. The judge asked for ____ in the court.
   - Ⓔ silence
   - Ⓖ scilents
   - Ⓕ slients
   - Ⓗ silints

5. The ____ was fifteen to twelve.
   - Ⓐ skor
   - Ⓒ skore
   - Ⓑ scoar
   - Ⓓ score

6. One ____ is another way of saying one fourth.
   - Ⓔ quiter
   - Ⓖ guitar
   - Ⓕ quarter
   - Ⓗ qaurter

GO ON TO NEXT PAGE ▸

Name _____ Date _____

Unit 3, lesson 1, page 2

7. Meg will be _____ working at 9 o'clock.
   - Ⓐ throught
   - Ⓑ trough
   - Ⓒ through
   - Ⓓ throuhg

8. Use a ruler to draw a _____ line.
   - Ⓔ strate
   - Ⓕ straight
   - Ⓖ straght
   - Ⓗ straigt

9. Terry returned the books to the _____.
   - Ⓐ libary
   - Ⓑ library
   - Ⓒ libury
   - Ⓓ librury

10. Tia mows the _____ every week.
    - Ⓔ lorn
    - Ⓕ lown
    - Ⓖ lone
    - Ⓗ lawn

11. My sister goes to an _____ class.
    - Ⓐ excercise
    - Ⓑ ecercise
    - Ⓒ exercize
    - Ⓓ exercise

12. Which ____ of the year do you like best?
    - Ⓔ season
    - Ⓕ seascon
    - Ⓖ seeson
    - Ⓗ seasen

STOP

Your time: _____

Number right: _____

On this lesson I did _____ because _____.

I think it would help me to _____.

Name _____   Date _____

Lesson 2: Using correct capitalization

DIRECTIONS ▶ Darken the circle for the part of the sentence that needs a capital letter. Darken the circle for *E. none* if the sentence <u>does not</u> need a capital letter.

💡 STRATEGY TIPS

1. Read each sentence.
2. Remember that capital letters are used for proper nouns (names of people, places, days, months), titles of people, books, stories, films, the word *I*, and the first word of a sentence or quotation.

Sample:

I want to	go to the	movies	on saturday.	none
Ⓐ	Ⓑ	Ⓒ	Ⓓ	Ⓔ

ANSWER

The correct answer is *D. on saturday.* Names of days of the week always start with a capital letter. *Saturday* should start with a capital letter.

✏️ NOW TRY THESE

1.
did	you watch	television	last night?	none
Ⓐ	Ⓑ	Ⓒ	Ⓓ	Ⓔ

2.
Jody said	to Tom,	"let's play	soccer."	none
Ⓐ	Ⓑ	Ⓒ	Ⓓ	Ⓔ

3.
We saw	mr. Green	at the store	today.	none
Ⓐ	Ⓑ	Ⓒ	Ⓓ	Ⓔ

4.
My	grandparents	live in	Montreal, Canada.	none
Ⓐ	Ⓑ	Ⓒ	Ⓓ	Ⓔ

GO ON TO NEXT PAGE ▶

Name_____   Date _____

Unit 3, lesson 2, page 2

5.   Jim's   favorite book   is   Black beauty.   none
     Ⓐ   Ⓑ   Ⓒ   Ⓓ   Ⓔ

6.   We go   back to   school   in september.   none
     Ⓐ   Ⓑ   Ⓒ   Ⓓ   Ⓔ

7.   Don's sister,   susan,   is a very   good singer.   none
     Ⓐ   Ⓑ   Ⓒ   Ⓓ   Ⓔ

8.   Why don't   you and i   make dinner   tonight?   none
     Ⓐ   Ⓑ   Ⓒ   Ⓓ   Ⓔ

9.   My family   went to   hawaii   last summer.   none
     Ⓐ   Ⓑ   Ⓒ   Ⓓ   Ⓔ

10.   Mrs. garcia   drove   Juan's friend   to school.   none
      Ⓐ   Ⓑ   Ⓒ   Ⓓ   Ⓔ

STOP

Your time: _____

Number right: _____

On this lesson I did _____ because _____
_____.

I think it would help me to _____
_____
_____.

Name_____ Date _____

Lesson 3: Using correct punctuation

DIRECTIONS ▶ Darken the circle for the punctuation mark that makes the sentence correct. Darken the circle for *E. none* if no punctuation mark is needed.

STRATEGY TIPS

1. As you read each sentence, think about the punctuation rules you use when you're writing.
2. What punctuation would you use on the sentences in this lesson?

Sample:
Do you want to go swimming
- Ⓐ .
- Ⓑ ;
- Ⓒ !
- Ⓓ ?
- Ⓔ none

ANSWER
The correct answer is *D. ?*. Always use a question mark to show that you are asking a question.

NOW TRY THESE

1. What time is it?" asked Jeff.
   - Ⓐ ?
   - Ⓑ ,
   - Ⓒ !
   - Ⓓ "
   - Ⓔ none

2. Beware of the dog
   - Ⓐ .
   - Ⓑ "
   - Ⓒ !
   - Ⓓ ;
   - Ⓔ none

3. You need eggs flour, and sugar to make a cake.
   - Ⓐ ,
   - Ⓑ "
   - Ⓒ "
   - Ⓓ !
   - Ⓔ none

4. Ellen wore her new hat, boots, and mittens.
   - Ⓐ ?
   - Ⓑ ;
   - Ⓒ .
   - Ⓓ ,
   - Ⓔ none

5. Please hand me the telephone book.
   - Ⓐ !
   - Ⓑ .
   - Ⓒ "
   - Ⓓ ,
   - Ⓔ none

6. Our teacher read <u>Where the Red Fern Grows</u> to the class.
   - Ⓐ "
   - Ⓑ ?
   - Ⓒ ,
   - Ⓓ !
   - Ⓔ none

7. Don't touch that sharp knife
   - Ⓐ ?
   - Ⓑ ;
   - Ⓒ .
   - Ⓓ !
   - Ⓔ none

8. Did you follow all the directions
   - Ⓐ .
   - Ⓑ ;
   - Ⓒ ?
   - Ⓓ "
   - Ⓔ none

GO ON TO NEXT PAGE ▶

© Steck-Vaughn Company   Test Taking 3, SV 6973-8

Name _____ Date _____

Unit 3, lesson 3, page 2

9. "What do you think of that" she asked.
   Ⓐ ? Ⓒ , Ⓔ none
   Ⓑ . Ⓓ "

10. It's too good to be true!
    Ⓐ ? Ⓒ ' Ⓔ none
    Ⓑ ; Ⓓ ,

11. I want to go too.
    Ⓐ ? Ⓒ " Ⓔ none
    Ⓑ , Ⓓ ;

12. Thank you for the gift
    Ⓐ ? Ⓒ , Ⓔ none
    Ⓑ . Ⓓ "

13. "Have a happy birthday! he exclaimed.
    Ⓐ . Ⓒ " Ⓔ none
    Ⓑ ? Ⓓ ,

14. Alaska is the largest state.
    Ⓐ ' Ⓒ , Ⓔ none
    Ⓑ " Ⓓ ?

STOP

Your time: _____

Number right: _____

On this lesson I did _____ because _____.

I think it would help me to _____

_____.

Name _____   Date _____

Lesson 4: Using correct capitalization and punctuation

DIRECTIONS ▸ Darken the circle for the sentence that shows correct capitalization and punctuation.

STRATEGY TIPS

1. In this lesson you will be looking for both capitalization and punctuation errors.
2. In each group of sentences below, only one sentence is correct.
3. As you read each sentence, think about the rules you have practiced.

Sample:
- Ⓐ There was snow on the ground!
- Ⓑ The oriole used string, and grass to build a nest.
- Ⓒ Aunt Jane is coming to visit next week.
- Ⓓ the pot of soup boiled over.

ANSWER

The correct answer is *C. Aunt Jane is coming to visit next week.* All the other sentences have a capitalization or punctuation error.

NOW TRY THESE

1. Ⓐ My dog duke chased the mailman.
   Ⓑ What is the name of the book you are reading.
   Ⓒ We're going to Washington D.C next week.
   Ⓓ Frank was excited about the trip he was to take.

2. Ⓔ They grow oranges, lemons, and grapes in the orchard.
   Ⓕ Mrs. james read a story to the class.
   Ⓖ My cousin lives in San Francisco?
   Ⓗ Judy is learning to knit!

3. Ⓐ Adam's birthday is november 12.
   Ⓑ Mary will visit us on Tuesday.
   Ⓒ We went to Disneyland last month
   Ⓓ Can you play the piano!

GO ON TO NEXT PAGE

Name_____   Date _____

Unit 3, lesson 4, page 2

4. Ⓔ we need warm clothes when we go sledding.
   Ⓕ March is a very windy, month.
   Ⓖ Did you ever visit Europe?
   Ⓗ Please don't touch that

5. Ⓐ Did you know they have a holiday called Doll Day in Japan?
   Ⓑ The fourth of July is a special day in the United States.
   Ⓒ There are many holidays in November;
   Ⓓ My favorite holiday is thanksgiving.

6. Ⓔ The North Star is called polaris.
   Ⓕ Sally said, "let's go for a walk."
   Ⓖ Stay away from fire!
   Ⓗ Russian people decorate eggs, for Easter.

7. Ⓐ Cal Ripken is a baseball hero.
   Ⓑ Magic johnson is a basketball hero.
   Ⓒ Which sport do you like best
   Ⓓ I like both baseball, and basketball.

8. Ⓔ <u>Curious George</u>, is a book about a funny monkey.
   Ⓕ Our last visit to the Zoo was fun!
   Ⓖ Yes Fred I'll go with you.
   Ⓗ No, I never saw that program.

9. Ⓐ Yesterday we went to the Museum.
   Ⓑ My favorite exhibit was of the Dinosaurs.
   Ⓒ The Brontosaurus skeleton was huge!
   Ⓓ We spent two hours there?

GO ON TO NEXT PAGE

© Steck-Vaughn Company   Test Taking 3, SV 6973-8

Name _____   Date _____

Unit 3, lesson 4, page 3

10. Ⓔ My Computer can do many things.
    Ⓕ I like to play games on the computer.
    Ⓖ It also, has a program that helps me with my homework
    Ⓗ I can draw pictures in the graphics program?

11. Ⓐ I painted a picture in Art Class.
    Ⓑ I used many different colors?
    Ⓒ Did you see it?
    Ⓓ Peter said, "That's a beautiful rainbow!

12. Ⓔ Todd and I played a game!
    Ⓕ I won Three times and he won Twice.
    Ⓖ We had a lot of fun.
    Ⓗ We will play again, soon

STOP

Your time: _____

Number right: _____

On this lesson I did _____ because _____

_____.

I think it would help me to _____

_____

_____.

Name_____   Date_____

PRACTICE TEST 3

Practice Test Answer Sheet, p. 96

Reminder: Read the directions before you start each part of the test. Study and think about the samples. Take your time!

Part 1

Directions: For questions 1–10, choose the correctly spelled word that completes each sentence. Record your answer on the answer sheet.

Sample: Cherries are my favorite _____.
  A frute   C fruit
  B firut   D frut

Answer: The correct answer is *C. fruit.* It is the only choice that is spelled correctly.

---

1. I read _____ good books last week.
   A four   C fuor
   B foar   D frou

2. Dan told us about his strange _____.
   A dreem   C dreme
   B drame   D dream

3. Can you _____ that high branch?
   A reatch   C reahc
   B reach   D reech

4. Do you like my new _____?
   A clothes   C klohes
   B close   D clohse

5. Long ago _____ roamed Earth.
   A dinosores C dinasaurs
   B dinosaurs D dinosaures

6. Jim _____ a huge fish last week.
   A caurt   C caught
   B cauht   D cawt

GO ON TO NEXT PAGE

© Steck-Vaughn Company   44   Test Taking 3, SV 6973-8

Name _____ Date _____

7. I like to read _____ tales.
   A fary   C fiary
   B fairey D fairy

8. We had to be very _____ during the show.
   A quiet C qute
   B queit D qeuit

9. That knife has a very sharp _____.
   A ege   C eddg
   B edge D edgh

10. I am my aunt's _____.
    A nece   C niece
    B neice D neece

Part 2

Directions: For questions 11–14, choose the part of the sentence that needs a capital letter. Choose *E. none* if no capital letter is needed. Record your answer on the answer sheet.

Sample:

The book	report is	due next	Thursday.	none
A	B	C	D	E

Answer: The correct answer is *E. none*. The sentence is correct as it is.

11. | Uncle jim | always brings | candy when | he visits. | none |
    | A | B | C | D | E |

12. | I went | to Jorge's | birthday | party yesterday. | none |
    | A | B | C | D | E |

13. | Sara said, | "my mother | bakes the | best cookies." | none |
    | A | B | C | D | E |

14. | I read | a very good | book by | Judy blume. | none |
    | A | B | C | D | E |

GO ON TO NEXT PAGE

Name_____ Date _____

Part 3

Directions: For questions 15–20, choose the punctuation mark that makes the sentence correct. Choose *E. none* if no punctuation mark is needed. Record your answer on the answer sheet.

Sample: Have you had your breakfast
 A ?   C '   E none
 B !   D ,

Answer: The correct answer is A. *?*. Questions should end with a question mark.

---

15. Doreen, please hand me the scissors
 A !   C .   E none
 B :   D ,

16. I don't like hamburgers
 A .   C ,   E none
 B "   D ?

17. Stay away from that angry dog
 A .   C ,   E none
 B !   D ?

18. *Star Trek* is a popular television show.
 A ,   C !   E none
 B ?   D .

19. When will you visit Paris, France
 A ,   C !   E none
 B .   D ?

20. James ordered cereal, eggs, and toast.
 A ?   C "   E none
 B ,   D .

GO ON TO NEXT PAGE

Name _____   Date _____

Part 4

Directions: For questions 21–24, choose the sentence that has correct capitalization and punctuation. Record your answer on the answer sheet.

Sample:
- A Did you ever visit Santa Fe, New Mexico
- B Babies like rattles blocks and balls.
- C Ms. holt is a great teacher!
- D How did you do that?

Answer: The correct answer is *D. How did you do that?* The other sentences have either incorrect capitalization or punctuation.

---

21. A I like to watch the olympics on TV.
    B I wish I could go to Atlanta Georgia.
    C Who do you think will win the most gold medals?
    D Ben Johnson of canada had to give his medals back.

22. A Deserts, are very dry places.
    B A dromedary is a kind of Camel.
    C Do you enjoy skiing?", asked Fran.
    D Terry, stop making all that noise!

23. A Do you think we'll send a spaceship to mars?
    B Jupiter is the largest of all the planets.
    C Jupiter, is 11 times as large as Earth!
    D When will we explore "Jupiter"?

24. A New York is called the Empire State.
    B which state is called the garden state?
    C My friend's aunt Sue is very pretty.
    D Tom please, pick up your toys.

STOP

Suggested Time Limit: 22 minutes   Your time: _____

Check your work if you have time. Wait for instructions from your teacher.

Name _____ Date _____

UNIT IV: READING COMPREHENSION

Lesson 1: Reading stories

DIRECTIONS ▶ Read the story. Darken the circle for the answer that best completes each sentence.

STRATEGY TIPS

1. Look at the questions before you read the story.
2. After you read the story, read the questions again.
3. Then read all the answer choices.
4. Some sentences are wrong because they are not true or are not mentioned in the paragraph.
5. Check your answers by looking back at the story.

Sample: Benjamin Franklin believed that lightning was the same as electricity. Most people thought that this was a foolish idea. Franklin flew a kite during a storm so he could get electricity from the lightning. He proved his theory was right.

Why did Franklin fly his kite during a storm?
Ⓐ He was a foolish man.
Ⓑ He wanted to prove his theory.
Ⓒ He was a clever man.
Ⓓ He thought that people were foolish.

ANSWER

The correct answer is *B. He wanted to prove his theory*. The second sentence in the story says that most people thought his idea was foolish. You can guess that he wanted to prove his theory.

NOW TRY THESE

Passage I

A banana field in blossom is a beautiful sight to see. It looks like a giant flower garden. The plants sometimes grow to a height of 25 feet! The purple blossoms can be as long as six to nine inches. The great drooping leaves are large and broad. Sometimes the leaves grow to be ten feet long and over two feet wide. They make a wonderful screen that shuts out the sunlight when it is too hot for the plant.

GO ON TO NEXT PAGE ▶

© Steck-Vaughn Company   48   Test Taking 3, SV 6973-8

Name _____ Date _____

Unit 4, lesson 1, page 2

1. To what does the author compare a banana field?
   - Ⓐ purple blossoms
   - Ⓑ drooping leaves
   - Ⓒ a giant flower garden
   - Ⓓ a wonderful screen

2. How do leaves protect the banana plant?
   - Ⓔ They are large and broad.
   - Ⓕ They keep the sun out.
   - Ⓖ They grow to be ten feet long.
   - Ⓗ They have large blossoms.

Passage II

Banana plants are not planted from seeds. New plants grow from small shoots beside the mature plants. The new plants grow rapidly. They reach their full height in one year. The blossoms appear when the plants are about nine months old. Each plant has one cluster of flowers from which one bunch of bananas will grow.

It takes about three or four months for the fruit to grow large enough to be cut. Bananas are always cut when they are green. If they are allowed to ripen on the plant, they lose their flavor and the skin bursts open. After the bunch of bananas is cut, the plant dies and is cut down. Then the new shoots grow up to take the place of the old plant, and the cycle begins again.

3. From this story we know that
   - Ⓐ bananas are never cut when they are green.
   - Ⓑ banana skin always bursts open.
   - Ⓒ bananas are always cut when they are ripe.
   - Ⓓ bananas are cut when they are green.

4. A good title for this story would be
   - Ⓔ Visiting a Banana Plantation.
   - Ⓕ The Life Cycle of Banana Plants.
   - Ⓖ How to Eat a Banana.
   - Ⓗ Bananas are Delicious.

GO ON TO NEXT PAGE

Name _____ Date _____

Unit 4, lesson 1, page 3

Passage III

The camp site, or location, was about five miles from the town. It was near a bay which was several miles wide. The bay was a good place for sailboats and motorboats. Near the camp site, a river emptied into the bay. The river was so calm that it was fine for rowboats, canoes, and kayaks.

The camp was set on a high point of land that reached out into the bay. There was a sandy beach that was great for swimming. Other places along the shore were low and muddy, with shallow water that was in the tall grass. That part was swampy and had many mosquitoes.

5. Another word for <u>location</u> is

    Ⓐ town.
    Ⓑ bay.
    Ⓒ shore.
    Ⓓ site.

6. You can guess that the campers probably

    Ⓔ had many cook-outs.
    Ⓕ had a boat race.
    Ⓖ did a lot of swimming and boating.
    Ⓗ went on long hikes.

7. The camp site was good because

    Ⓐ you could see all kinds of boats.
    Ⓑ it was away from the swampy water.
    Ⓒ it was near good hiking trails.
    Ⓓ tall grass grew in the mud.

GO ON TO NEXT PAGE

Name _____   Date _____

Unit 4, lesson 1, page 4

Passage IV

Most beavers live in lodges that they build in small streams. The lodges are made of sticks and mud. Some of them are several feet high. The lodge is always built so that a part of it stands above the water, though the entrance is always under the water.

The beavers build a dam to make a pond in the stream. The dam keeps the water around the lodge from getting too high or too low. A beaver dam is always made near woods. When trees are cut down, they must be near enough to fall into the water. The trees are used to build the lodges and dams. Beavers can cut down small trees with their sharp teeth. They know how to cut them so they fall into the water.

Birch tree bark is the main part of the beaver's diet. During the summer the beavers cut a great many short pieces of birch wood. They sink them in their ponds by covering them with mud. Then, when winter comes and the pond freezes over, they have plenty of bark to eat.

8. You can tell that beavers are very
   - Ⓔ playful.
   - Ⓕ hungry.
   - Ⓖ lazy.
   - Ⓗ clever.

9. Beaver dams are made near woods because
   - Ⓐ the wood is softer.
   - Ⓑ there are many animals.
   - Ⓒ the trees can fall into the water after they are cut.
   - Ⓓ the ground is muddy.

10. A beaver lodge is a kind of
    - Ⓔ tree.
    - Ⓕ water.
    - Ⓖ nest.
    - Ⓗ mud.

11. The beaver probably builds the entrance to his lodge underwater because
    - Ⓐ he can escape from his enemies.
    - Ⓑ he can swim faster.
    - Ⓒ he can find more food.
    - Ⓓ he can cut down small trees.

GO ON TO NEXT PAGE

Name _____   Date _____

Unit 4, lesson 1, page 5

Passage V

In the winter most birds fly south so they can live in warmer climates. Birds have been known to fly nonstop across oceans and seas. These flights may not be reported in the news, but they are quite amazing. Just think about how tiny some of these birds are!

One bird, the arctic tern, nests near the North Pole. When their fledglings are old enough, the arctic terns fly to islands near the South Pole. They cross many oceans and many lands. In fact, they spend about half their lives flying.

Robins and bluebirds don't fly so far. They spend their winters in the middle states. Orioles and tiny hummingbirds fly down to Mexico and Central America.

12. According to the story, it is amazing that

   - Ⓔ arctic terns live near the North Pole.
   - Ⓕ robins and bluebirds fly to the middle states.
   - Ⓖ tiny birds can fly nonstop across the ocean.
   - Ⓗ hummingbirds fly down to Mexico.

13. Another word for *fledglings* could be

   - Ⓐ babies.
   - Ⓑ mothers.
   - Ⓒ fathers.
   - Ⓓ parents.

14. From this passage you can guess that the birds that make the longest flights are

   - Ⓔ robins.
   - Ⓕ arctic terns.
   - Ⓖ bluebirds.
   - Ⓗ hummingbirds.

15. A good title for this story is

   - Ⓐ Birds That Make Nonstop Ocean Flights.
   - Ⓑ When Birds Fly South.
   - Ⓒ Where Some Birds Spend the Winter.
   - Ⓓ The Arctic Tern's Long Flight.

GO ON TO NEXT PAGE

Name _____ Date _____

Unit 4, lesson 1, page 6

Passage VI

A little match can be a dangerous thing. It could set an entire forest on fire. In the Pacific Northwest alone, over 300,000 acres were blackened by forest fires in 1929. Thousands of animals were killed. Many homes were destroyed, and millions of dollars were lost just in that one year.

The fire broke out in September when the forest was very dry. The fire was caused by some careless campers. They dropped lighted matches in the dry woods. Before they knew it, fire was raging through the forest. Nothing was left of the beautiful forest but ugly, black stumps.

Nowadays, camps and parks have signs warning people to be careful when using matches. They want to prevent forest fires. The signs usually have a picture of a bear dressed in a forest ranger uniform. The bear's name is Smokey.

16. According to the story
    - E 300,000 acres of forest are blackened by fire each year.
    - F campers deliberately set the fire.
    - G 300,000 acres were blackened by fire in 1929.
    - H millions of animals were killed.

17. You can tell that
    - A forest fires are still a problem today.
    - B Smokey likes to wear his ranger uniform.
    - C there are many careless campers.
    - D there's no way to prevent forest fires.

GO ON TO NEXT PAGE

Name _____   Date _____

Unit 4, lesson 1, page 7

Passage VII

Paul and his friends went to explore the woods. As they walked down a path, Paul noticed a large blackberry bush. He decided to pick some berries for a snack.

Just as Paul reached in to pick some berries, he heard a soft "Coo-coo-coo." He listened carefully and started to look around to see if he could find where the sound was coming from. Suddenly a gray bird fell to the ground. It was flopping about. Paul thought that the bird had a broken wing so he stooped to pick up the bird. But it flopped just ahead of him. So Paul followed the bird. When they were far away from the bush, it flew away.

Paul went back to the blackberry bush. He saw two beautiful white eggs in a nest no higher than his head. He didn't touch the eggs, and Paul and his friends decided to look for another blackberry bush.

Later they saw the bird fly back to her nest. They could hear her saying "Coo-coo-coo," as though she was glad her nest had not been disturbed.

18. Paul reached into the bush because he
    - E saw a bird's nest.
    - F wanted to pick blackberries.
    - G heard a strange sound.
    - H wanted to help the bird.

19. From the story you can guess the mother bird
    - A was worried about the eggs in her nest.
    - B didn't want Paul to pick berries.
    - C had a broken wing.
    - D wanted to build another nest.

20. The mother bird probably
    - E wanted the berries for herself.
    - F pretended that her wing was broken.
    - G had been sitting there a long time.
    - H couldn't fly very far.

21. A good title for this story would be
    - A Paul and His Friends.
    - B Let's Go Explore.
    - C How to Pick Berries.
    - D A Clever Bird.

STOP

Your time: _____

Number right: _____

Name _____   Date _____

Lesson 2: Choosing titles

DIRECTIONS ▶ Darken the circle for the best title for each paragraph.

STRATEGY TIPS
1. Read all the sentences in the paragraph.
2. Decide what they have in common.
3. Choose the best title for each paragraph.

Sample: Jan read a story about an elf. There was a picture of the elf in the book. The picture showed the elf dressed in a black coat, knee breeches, and a broad-brimmed black hat. The elf's face was old and wrinkled. He was searching for something in a strange-looking chest. Jan turned the page quickly to find out what the elf found in the chest.

Ⓐ Reading a Silly Story
Ⓑ What Elves Look Like
Ⓒ A Story About an Elf
Ⓓ Searching for Treasure

ANSWER

The correct answer is *C. A Story About an Elf.* Each sentence in the paragraph tells about an elf.

NOW TRY THESE

1. In the summer the sheep are washed in clean water. Then, as soon as the wool is dry, it is sheared off the sheep. The wool from each sheep holds together as a mat. The wool is called fleece. If the wool is cut early in the summer, the sheep can grow new fleece. Then they will be warm in the winter.

    Ⓐ How Wool Is Cut
    Ⓑ Caring for Sheep
    Ⓒ Weaving a Mat
    Ⓓ Keeping Warm

2. Camels store food and water in the strangest way. They store food in the two humps on their backs. They store water in their two stomachs! When they go on long journeys across the desert, they always have their food and water with them.

    Ⓔ Crossing The Desert
    Ⓕ The Camel's Hump
    Ⓖ Strange Animals
    Ⓗ How Camels Store Food and Water

GO ON TO NEXT PAGE

Name _____   Date _____

Unit 4, lesson 2, page 2

3. Humans are different from animals in many ways. Animals do not think the way humans do. Humans are able to solve problems. They can also figure out ways to do new things. Animals cannot do this.

    Ⓐ The Way Animals Think
    Ⓑ How Humans and Animals Differ
    Ⓒ Thinking of New Things
    Ⓓ Solving Problems

4. There are many different kinds of farms. One kind of farm is a dairy farm. Dairy farmers raise cows for milk. In the summer the cows graze in the fields. They are brought in to be milked twice a day. The milk is then shipped to dairy companies. The milk is put into bottles and cartons, then it is shipped to stores.

    Ⓔ All Kinds of Farms
    Ⓕ Summer on the Farm
    Ⓖ Shipping the Milk
    Ⓗ From Farm to Store

5. The women at the fort collected white shirts, blue coats, and red coats. They cut stars and stripes from the clothes. Quickly they stitched them together to make the American flag. When it was finished, they raised it over the fort to cheer the people.

    Ⓐ Making New Clothes
    Ⓑ Life at a Fort
    Ⓒ Making a Flag
    Ⓓ Brave People

Your time: _____

Number right: _____

On this lesson I did _____ because _____

_____.

Name _____ Date _____

Lesson 3: Arranging sentences in correct order
Part one

DIRECTIONS ▶ Darken the circle for the sentence which should come <u>first</u> in each of the following groups of sentences.

STRATEGY TIPS

1. When you read the sentences, look for signal words such as *first, next, later, so,* and *then*.
2. They will help you decide the correct order for the sentences.

Sample

Ⓐ Then it is harvest time.

Ⓑ The seeds begin growing as they get sun and water.

Ⓒ At planting time, farmers work long hours to plant seeds.

Ⓓ Several months later, the crops are fully grown.

ANSWER

The correct answer is *C. At planting time, farmers work long hours to plant seeds.* The other sentences tell what happens after the seeds are planted.

NOW TRY THESE

1. Ⓐ In colonial times, people had to think of ways to entertain themselves at home.

   Ⓑ So, we know that colonial children never watched television.

   Ⓒ They read books, played games, or played musical instruments.

   Ⓓ The kinds of home entertainment we have were not invented yet.

2. Ⓔ Therefore, people who live in this zone do not need to buy warm clothing.

   Ⓕ It is very hot there.

   Ⓖ The equator is an imaginary line around the earth.

   Ⓗ Countries near the equator are in the torrid zone.

GO ON TO NEXT PAGE

Name _____ Date _____

Unit 4, lesson 3, part 1, page 2

3. Ⓐ As a result, we have many different cultures in our cities.

   Ⓑ People have come here from all over the world.

   Ⓒ They were looking for a better life.

   Ⓓ The United States is a nation of immigrants.

4. Ⓔ He is known as one of America's best poets.

   Ⓕ Langston Hughes' poems are enjoyed by many people.

   Ⓖ His poems are mostly about ordinary African-American life.

   Ⓗ He wrote about his experiences in Harlem.

5. Ⓐ Some people like to go to spas for their vacation.

   Ⓑ They like the healthy food served there.

   Ⓒ They think the spa program will make them healthy.

   Ⓓ They like the exercise training.

6. Ⓔ It shines very brightly.

   Ⓕ It is easy to find it in the sky.

   Ⓖ It is above the North Pole.

   Ⓗ Sailors use the North Star to tell which way is north.

STOP

Your time: _____

Number right: _____

On this lesson I did _____ because _____

_____.

I think it would help me to _____

_____

_____.

Name _____   Date _____

Lesson 3: Arranging sentences in correct order Part two

DIRECTIONS ▸ Darken the circle of the sentence which should come <u>last</u> in each of the following groups of sentences.

STRATEGY TIP Remember to look for the signal words.

NOW TRY THESE

7. Ⓐ Then, they are painted with bright colors.
   Ⓑ Native Americans have unique customs.
   Ⓒ First, the poles are carved like animal heads and faces of people.
   Ⓓ Many Indian tribes make special totem poles for their communities.

8. Ⓔ After two long days, the storm was over.
   Ⓕ Then, snow began to fall, and the wind grew stonger.
   Ⓖ It started with a strong wind.
   Ⓗ Last year there was a terrible blizzard in New York.

9. Ⓐ Sometimes weather forecasters use special balloons to study the weather.
   Ⓑ Then, they take these machines back to the lab.
   Ⓒ They hook machines to the balloons and send them up to the sky.
   Ⓓ When the balloons pop, the machines fall to earth.

10. Ⓔ Blind people read from special books written in Braille.
    Ⓕ Braille letters are made of raised dots on the page.
    Ⓖ The letters are read by touching the dots.
    Ⓗ Louis Braille invented this method of reading and changed the lives of many blind people.

STOP

Name _____   Date _____

PRACTICE TEST 4

Practice Test Answer Sheet, p. 95

Part 1

Directions: For questions 1–10, choose the answer that best completes each sentence about the story. Record your answer on the answer sheet.

Sample: The United States Civil War is sometimes referred to as the battle of the Blue and the Gray. Those were the colors of the uniforms worn by the two armies.

These two armies fought for several years. Finally, the war came to an end when General Lee surrendered to General Grant at Appomatox Courthouse. At last the country was united again.

From the story you can tell that the war
A was over quickly.
B lasted a long time.
C was won by the South.
D had many brave generals.

Answer: The correct answer is *B. lasted a long time.* The other choices are not true or are not mentioned in the story.

Passage 1

Trees are a natural resource. After they are cut down, trees are cut into logs and planks of wood. The wood is used to build houses and to make furniture. It is also used to make paper.

Many other products come from trees. Syrup from maple trees is used to sweeten food. Sap from other trees is used to make paint and ink.

People must not be wasteful of the products that come from trees. If we conserve, this resource will last longer.

1. **In this story the word *conserve* means**
   A to waste.
   B to save.
   C to use.
   D to ship.

2. **From this story you can tell that trees**
   E grow very tall.
   F give us lots of maple syrup.
   G are not very useful.
   H are an important resource.

GO ON TO NEXT PAGE

Name _____ Date _____

Passage II

Washington, D.C., our nation's capital, is a beautiful city. It has wide avenues and tree-lined streets. Millions of tourists visit the city each year. Some of the buildings that people visit are the Smithsonian Institution, the Supreme Court, the FBI building, the U.S. Mint, and the White House.

The U.S. Capitol is one of the buildings that most tourists visit. Both houses of Congress are in the Capitol. One section of the building is for the House of Representatives. The other section is for the Senate. The rotunda, in the center of the building under the dome, separates the sections.

3. **You can tell that the author thinks**
   A everyone should visit the FBI building.
   B Washington, D.C., is a good place to visit.
   C most tourists like the White House best.
   D the Supreme Court is a special building.

4. **The Congress of the United States**
   E has many buildings.
   F works at the White House.
   G meets in the rotunda.
   H is made up of two parts.

5. **A building not listed is the**
   A Smithsonian.
   B White House.
   C Library of Congress.
   D U.S. Mint.

6. **From this passage you can tell that the rotunda is a**
   E circular area in the U.S. Capitol.
   F building to visit in Washington, D.C.
   G room inside the House of Representatives.
   H part of the Supreme Court.

GO ON TO NEXT PAGE

Name _____   Date _____

Passage III

Peter was not having a good day. His team wasn't having a good day, either. They were losing the game. It was the bottom of the ninth inning. His team had two outs, and runners were on second and third base.

Peter stepped up to the plate and waited for the pitch. Thwack! He had just hit a double and was now safe on second base.

The next batter at the plate struck out. But it didn't matter. Who said this wasn't *his* lucky day?

7. Peter's team was unhappy because

A they were losing.
B it was the end of the game.
C they had no runners on base.
D Peter struck out.

8. Peter probably felt proud when

E the batter struck out.
F his team lost.
G he had a bad day.
H he hit a double.

9. When the game was over, Peter probably

A went to first base.
B ran to home plate.
C felt very happy.
D ran out on the field.

10. A good title for this story could be

E Ninth Inning Problem.
F Running Home.
G An Unhappy Team.
H A Lucky Day After All.

GO ON TO NEXT PAGE

Name _____   Date _____

Part 2

Directions: For questions 11–12, choose the letter for the best title for each paragraph. Record your answer on the answer sheet.

Sample: In the fall, leaves turn many colors. The reds, yellows, and browns look like a beautiful painting. They look especially beautiful near evergreens.

- A Beautiful Evergreens
- B Leaves in Fall
- C Red, Yellows, and Browns
- D Painting Pretty Woods

Answer: The correct answer is *B. Leaves in Fall*. Each sentence in the paragraph tells about leaves in fall.

---

11. We had been waiting on the sidewalk for a long time. Suddenly we heard a band playing. Many colorful floats came behind the band. All of the people on the floats waved to the crowd.

- A Watching a Parade
- B Waiting on the Sidewalk
- C Waving to the Crowd
- D Floating Down the Avenue

12. The loaves in pans move on a special belt to the steam box. As the pans go slowly through the steam box, the dough gets lighter. When the loaves are ready to be baked, they go to the oven. Bread is taken from the oven when it has baked.

- E The Steam Box
- F Making Dough Lighter
- G Many Loaves of Bread
- H How Bread Is Baked

GO ON TO NEXT PAGE

Name _____   Date _____

Part 3

Directions: For questions 13–16, choose the letter for the sentence which should come <u>first</u> in each paragraph. Record your answer on the answer sheet.

Sample:
- A Then, he rested his head on the desk.
- B He covered his mouth with his hand as he yawned.
- C He leaned back on his chair and stretched his arms.
- D Manuel was very tired.

Answer: The correct answer is *D. Manuel was very tired.* The other sentences give details that show he was very tired.

13.
- A Each plant is set in its muddy bed by hand.
- B The farmer is barefoot as he walks in the wet fields.
- C In Asia rice is grown in large, wet fields.
- D The rice fields are called paddies.

14.
- E The potatoes were ready to be harvested from the ground.
- F The machine stuck its iron fingers down under the potato plants.
- G They used the new potato digger.
- H It lifted out a clump of dirt and potatoes.

15.
- A Next spring their buds will open and grow into leaves.
- B The bare trees are now ready for winter.
- C Food is stored in their roots and branches.
- D The leaves will give us summer shade.

16.
- E For this reason cities lay underground pipes for their water supply.
- F In the city it would not be possible to get enough water this way.
- G The pipes can carry the water as far as 100 miles.
- H In the country people get water from wells and springs.

GO ON TO NEXT PAGE

© Steck-Vaughn Company   Test Taking 3, SV 6973-8

Name _____   Date _____

Part 3 (cont.)

Directions: For questions 17–20, choose the letter for the sentence which should come <u>last</u> in the paragraph. Record your answer on the answer sheet.

Sample:
- A He threw something silvery on the river bank.
- B The bear had caught a fish with his big, hairy paw.
- C The bear kept his eyes on the water.
- D Then, quick as a wink, his paw struck the water.

Answer: The correct answer is B. *The bear had caught a fish with his big, hairy paw.* This sentence best completes the paragraph.

17.
- A No one lives in these rooms.
- B The President of the U.S. lives and works in the White House.
- C Many of the rooms in the White House are used for government business.
- D Some of the rooms are offices for the President's staff.

18.
- E It was used to pick seeds from cotton fiber.
- F Before his invention most workers could not clean more than a pound of cotton a day.
- G Eli Whitney invented the cotton gin.
- H A large cotton gin could clean as much cotton in a day as ten people could do by hand.

19.
- A She represented hope.
- B It was the Statue of Liberty.
- C In 1886 the people of France gave the United States a very special gift.
- D Today, more than one hundred years later, Miss Liberty is still a symbol of freedom to the world.

20.
- E His trip created a sensation.
- F It created an interest in airplanes as a way to travel.
- G Charles Lindbergh was the first person to fly alone from New York to Paris.
- H Today, people fly all around the world.

STOP

Name _____   Date _____

UNIT V: MATH PRACTICE

Lesson 1: Using number concepts

DIRECTIONS ▸ Darken the circle for the correct answer. Darken the circle for *E. none* if the correct answer is <u>not given</u>.

STRATEGY TIPS

1. Look for key words or symbols in the question and in the choices.
2. Make sure your answer fits with these.
3. Read all the choices.

Sample:

Which of the numbers has a 4 in the hundreds place?

- Ⓐ 2,634
- Ⓑ 3,490
- Ⓒ 7,054
- Ⓓ 4,138
- Ⓔ none

ANSWER

The correct answer is *B. 3,490*. The key words in the question are *4* and *hundreds*.

NOW TRY THESE

1. Which of these is an even number?
   - Ⓐ 75
   - Ⓑ 214
   - Ⓒ 999
   - Ⓓ 47
   - Ⓔ none

2. Which of these is the Roman numeral for 17?
   - Ⓐ XVI
   - Ⓑ IXIV
   - Ⓒ XVII
   - Ⓓ VXII
   - Ⓔ none

3. What does the 6 in 6,423 mean?
   - Ⓐ six hundred
   - Ⓑ six thousand
   - Ⓒ sixty
   - Ⓓ six
   - Ⓔ none

4. Which of these is equal to 825?
   - Ⓐ 80 + 25
   - Ⓑ 200 + 85
   - Ⓒ 8 + 250
   - Ⓓ 800 + 125
   - Ⓔ none

GO ON TO NEXT PAGE ▸

© Steck-Vaughn Company   Test Taking 3, SV 6973-8

Unit 5, lesson 1, page 2

5. Which of these sentences is correct?
   - Ⓐ 8 > 9
   - Ⓑ 146 < 223
   - Ⓒ 78 > 80
   - Ⓓ 561 < 446
   - Ⓔ none

6. Which point is 30 on the number line?

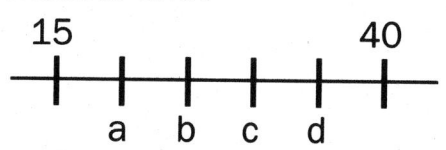

   15 ———————— 40
       a b c d

   - Ⓐ a
   - Ⓑ b
   - Ⓒ c
   - Ⓓ d
   - Ⓔ none

7. What is the missing number in this number series?

   6, 9, 12, ___, 18

   - Ⓐ 13
   - Ⓑ 15
   - Ⓒ 17
   - Ⓓ 0
   - Ⓔ none

8. Which clock shows 6:15?

   a. [clock]   c. [clock]
   b. [clock]   d. [clock]

   - Ⓐ a
   - Ⓑ b
   - Ⓒ c
   - Ⓓ d
   - Ⓔ none

9. Which of these equals 5?
   - Ⓐ 0 x 5
   - Ⓑ 5 − 1
   - Ⓒ 5 + 0
   - Ⓓ 5 x 5
   - Ⓔ none

10. How would you round 726 to the nearest ten?
    - Ⓐ 730
    - Ⓑ 720
    - Ⓒ 736
    - Ⓓ 725
    - Ⓔ none

GO ON TO NEXT PAGE

Name _____   Date _____

Unit 5, lesson 1, page 3

11. Which number makes both number sentences true?

    3 X 3 = ___   ___ + 3 = 12

    Ⓐ 6
    Ⓑ 9
    Ⓒ 8
    Ⓓ 0
    Ⓔ none

12. What is the pattern?

    1, 2, 4, 8, 16

    Ⓐ + 2
    Ⓑ x 2
    Ⓒ x 4
    Ⓓ + 4
    Ⓔ none

13. What time is 5 hours after 10:00 PM?

    Ⓐ 1:00 AM
    Ⓑ 5:00 AM
    Ⓒ 3:00 AM
    Ⓓ 3:00 PM
    Ⓔ none

14. Which would make this sentence correct?

    17 ___ 15

    Ⓐ >
    Ⓑ <
    Ⓒ =
    Ⓓ :
    Ⓔ none

STOP

Your time: _____

Number right: _____

On this lesson I did _____ because _____

_____.

I think it would help me to _____

_____.

Name _____   Date _____

Lesson 2: Using mixed operations
Part one

DIRECTIONS ▶ Darken the circle for the operation that makes each number sentence true.

STRATEGY TIPS

1. First, read the part of the equation that <u>does not</u> have a blank.
2. Then try each sign in the blank to find the one that makes the equation true.

Sample:

3 + 4 = 1 __ 7

Ⓐ +
Ⓑ −
Ⓒ ×
Ⓓ ÷

ANSWER

The correct answer is *C. x.*
1 x 7 is the same as *3 + 4*.

NOW TRY THESE

1. 4 + 5 = 3 __ 3
   Ⓐ +
   Ⓑ −
   Ⓒ ×
   Ⓓ ÷

2. 12 − 5 = 35 __ 5
   Ⓔ +
   Ⓕ −
   Ⓖ ×
   Ⓗ ÷

3. 48 __ 8 = 35 + 5
   Ⓐ +
   Ⓑ −
   Ⓒ ×
   Ⓓ ÷

4. 30 __ 6 = 27 + 9
   Ⓔ +
   Ⓕ −
   Ⓖ ×
   Ⓗ ÷

5. 7 __ 4 = 9 ÷ 3
   Ⓐ +
   Ⓑ −
   Ⓒ ×
   Ⓓ ÷

6. 3 __ 2 = 14 − 8
   Ⓔ +
   Ⓕ −
   Ⓖ ×
   Ⓗ ÷

GO ON TO NEXT PAGE

Name _____   Date _____

Unit 5, lesson 2, part 1, page 2

7. 5 x 5 = 30 __ 5
   - Ⓐ +
   - Ⓑ −
   - Ⓒ x
   - Ⓓ ÷

8. 2 __ 2 = 6 − 2
   - Ⓔ +
   - Ⓕ −
   - Ⓖ x
   - Ⓗ ÷

9. 3 __ 1 = 12 ÷ 4
   - Ⓐ +
   - Ⓑ −
   - Ⓒ x
   - Ⓓ ÷

10. 28 __ 7 = 3 + 1
    - Ⓔ +
    - Ⓕ −
    - Ⓖ x
    - Ⓗ ÷

11. 10 __ 10 = 10 x 0
    - Ⓐ +
    - Ⓑ −
    - Ⓒ x
    - Ⓓ ÷

12. 20 ÷ 5 = 12 __ 3
    - Ⓔ +
    - Ⓕ −
    - Ⓖ x
    - Ⓗ ÷

STOP

Your time: _____

Number right: _____

On this lesson I did _____ because _____

_____ .

I think it would help me to _____

_____ .

Name _____   Date _____

Lesson 2: Using mixed operations
Part two

DIRECTIONS Darken the circle for the correct answer. Darken the circle for *E. none* if the correct answer is **not given**.

STRATEGY TIPS

1. Always look at the sign to make sure you are doing the correct operation.
2. When regrouping, work the problem on scrap paper.
3. Estimate the answer.
4. Cross out any choices that must be wrong.

Sample:

```
  2,642
-    79
```

Ⓐ 2,721
Ⓑ 2,663
Ⓒ 2,563
Ⓓ 3,563
Ⓔ none

ANSWER

The correct answer is *C. 2,563*. Since you need to subtract, you could cross out any number larger than 2,642.

NOW TRY THESE

13.
```
  57
 +63
```
Ⓐ 110
Ⓑ 120
Ⓒ 130
Ⓓ 111
Ⓔ none

14. 7)̄56
Ⓐ 9
Ⓑ 5
Ⓒ 7
Ⓓ 49
Ⓔ none

15.
```
  378
 -205
```
Ⓐ 683
Ⓑ 573
Ⓒ 173
Ⓓ 163
Ⓔ none

16.
```
  21
x  4
```
Ⓐ 84
Ⓑ 25
Ⓒ 65
Ⓓ 64
Ⓔ none

GO ON TO NEXT PAGE

Name _____   Date _____

Unit 5, lesson 2, part 2, page 2

17. 53
    x 3

Ⓐ 1,509
Ⓑ 159
Ⓒ 156
Ⓓ   86
Ⓔ none

21. 6)̄42

Ⓐ 6
Ⓑ 7
Ⓒ 8
Ⓓ 9
Ⓔ none

18. 7)̄52

Ⓐ 5
Ⓑ 6
Ⓒ 7 R3
Ⓓ 6 R6
Ⓔ none

22.   12
    x 8

Ⓐ 46
Ⓑ 96
Ⓒ 92
Ⓓ 84
Ⓔ none

19. 3,271
    − 1,805

Ⓐ 2,466
Ⓑ 2,674
Ⓒ 42,474
Ⓓ 1,466
Ⓔ none

23. 112
     234
   + 108

Ⓐ 434
Ⓑ 348
Ⓒ 454
Ⓓ 588
Ⓔ none

20. 397
     257
   + 603

Ⓐ 1,611
Ⓑ 1,257
Ⓒ 1,247
Ⓓ 1,157
Ⓔ none

24. 5,827
    − 391

Ⓐ 4,576
Ⓑ 5,436
Ⓒ 5,276
Ⓓ 4,218
Ⓔ none

GO ON TO NEXT PAGE

Name _____ Date _____

Unit 5, lesson 2, part 2, page 3

Add or subtract to solve:

25. Mark went on a 225-mile bicycle trip. He rode 36 miles the first day. How many more miles did he have to go?

    Ⓐ 220 miles
    Ⓑ 189 miles
    Ⓒ 261 miles
    Ⓓ 181 miles
    Ⓔ none

26. A baker used 230 pounds of flour to bake bread. He used another 165 pounds of flour to bake cakes. How many pounds of flour did he use in all?

    Ⓐ 435
    Ⓑ 395
    Ⓒ 335
    Ⓓ 490
    Ⓔ none

27. In the school election, Carol got 57 votes from the third grade, 14 votes from the fourth grade, and 35 votes from the fifth grade. How many votes did she get in all?

    Ⓐ 96
    Ⓑ 78
    Ⓒ 106
    Ⓓ 121
    Ⓔ none

28. The cafeteria serves 247 students in the first lunch period and 369 students in the second lunch period. How many students are served in both lunch periods?

    Ⓐ 561
    Ⓑ 549
    Ⓒ 643
    Ⓓ 616
    Ⓔ none

GO ON TO NEXT PAGE

Name _____ Date _____

Unit 5, lesson 2, part 2, page 4

Multiply or divide to solve:

29. Maya has 24 model cars. She plans to arrange them in groups of 4. How many groups will she have in all?

   Ⓐ 5 groups
   Ⓑ 2 groups
   Ⓒ 6 groups
   Ⓓ 96 groups
   Ⓔ none

30. Jay's mystery book is 144 pages long. Each chapter has 12 pages. How many chapters are in Jay's mystery book?

   Ⓐ 24
   Ⓑ 12
   Ⓒ 18
   Ⓓ 9
   Ⓔ none

31. Andra is making microwave popcorn to share while watching movies with friends. Each box has 4 bags of popcorn. If each person eats 1 bag of popcorn, how many boxes of popcorn does Andra need for 10 people?

   Ⓐ 7
   Ⓑ 3
   Ⓒ 2
   Ⓓ 10
   Ⓔ none

32. The golf coach gave 6 players the same number of golf balls. After Tim hit 4 golf balls, he had 3 left. How many golf balls in all did the coach give the players?

   Ⓐ 36
   Ⓑ 42
   Ⓒ 24
   Ⓓ 72
   Ⓔ none

STOP

Your time: _____

Number right: _____

On this lesson I did _____ because _____

_____.

Name _____   Date _____

Lesson 3: Using fractions and decimals

DIRECTIONS ▶ Darken the circle for the correct answer to each question. Darken the circle for *E. none* if the correct answer is not given.

STRATEGY TIPS
1. Remember that fractions and decimals are ways of naming a part of a whole or a group.
2. Look for key words or symbols.
3. Remember to line up decimal points when you are adding or subtracting.
4. Estimate the answer.
5. Cross out any choices that must be wrong.

Sample:
What is the lowest term of $\frac{8}{16}$?

Ⓐ $\frac{1}{3}$ Ⓒ $\frac{2}{3}$ Ⓔ none

Ⓑ $\frac{1}{2}$ Ⓓ $\frac{2}{4}$

ANSWER
The correct answer is $B. \frac{1}{2}$.
The key words are *lowest term*.

NOW TRY THESE

1. Which is the decimal for this picture?

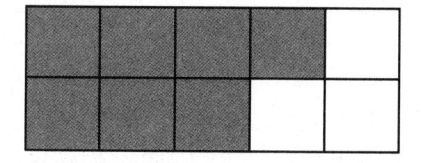

   Ⓐ 0.4
   Ⓑ 3.0
   Ⓒ 0.3
   Ⓓ 0.7
   Ⓔ none

2. Which words tell about this picture?

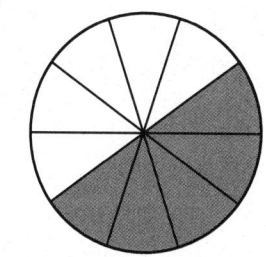

   Ⓐ three tenths
   Ⓑ eight tenths
   Ⓒ five tenths
   Ⓓ six tenths
   Ⓔ none

GO ON TO NEXT PAGE

© Steck-Vaughn Company   Test Taking 3, SV 6973-8

Name _____ Date _____

Unit 5, lesson 3, page 2

3. What is an equivalent fraction of $\frac{1}{4}$?

   Ⓐ $\frac{2}{8}$ Ⓒ $\frac{4}{8}$ Ⓔ none

   Ⓑ $\frac{1}{2}$ Ⓓ $\frac{3}{8}$

4. $\frac{9}{4}$ =

   Ⓐ $3\frac{2}{4}$ Ⓒ $1\frac{2}{4}$ Ⓔ none

   Ⓑ $2\frac{2}{4}$ Ⓓ $2\frac{1}{4}$

5. Which number shows three tenths?

   Ⓐ 30   Ⓒ 0.03   Ⓔ none
   Ⓑ 0.3   Ⓓ 3

6. 0.5 + 0.4 =

   Ⓐ 0.1   Ⓒ 9   Ⓔ none
   Ⓑ 0.10   Ⓓ 1

7. 0.9 − 0.7 =

   Ⓐ 0.4   Ⓒ 0.6   Ⓔ none
   Ⓑ 0.2   Ⓓ 0.3

8. Seven tenths − three tenths =

   Ⓐ 0.5   Ⓒ 0.4   Ⓔ none
   Ⓑ 0.2   Ⓓ 0.1

9. 3.7 =

   Ⓐ 3.07   Ⓒ 3.70   Ⓔ none
   Ⓑ 10   Ⓓ 37

10. $ .62
    − $ .38

    Ⓐ $0.36   Ⓒ $1.00   Ⓔ none
    Ⓑ $0.24   Ⓓ $0.26

STOP

Your time: _____

Number right: _____

On this lesson I did _____ because _____

_____.

I think it would help me to _____

_____.

Name _____ Date _____

Lesson 4: Using geometry and measurement

DIRECTIONS ▶ Darken the circle for the correct answer.

STRATEGY TIPS
1. Use the pictures of the objects to help you answer each question.
2. Remember: Perimeter is the measurement around the outside of a shape.
3. Area is the measurement of the space inside an object.

Sample A:
What is the perimeter of this rectangle?

Ⓐ 32 inches
Ⓑ 16 inches
Ⓒ 24 inches
Ⓓ 12 inches

8 in
4 in

ANSWER
The correct answer is *C. 24 inches*. Add the length of all sides of a figure to find the perimeter.

Sample B:
Which is the most reasonable estimate of the length of a hiking trail?

Ⓔ 3 kilometers
Ⓕ 12 millimeters
Ⓖ 6 meters
Ⓗ 200 centimeters

ANSWER
The correct answer is *A. 3 kilometers*. The other choices are not reasonable measurements of the length of a hiking trail.

NOW TRY THESE

1. What unit of measurement would you use to fill a swimming pool?

   Ⓐ cup
   Ⓑ gallon
   Ⓒ quart
   Ⓓ pint

2. How much time passes between 4:10 P.M. and 6:45 P.M.?

   Ⓔ 2 hours 30 minutes
   Ⓕ 4 hours
   Ⓖ 2 hours 35 minutes
   Ⓗ 1 hour 40 minutes

GO ON TO NEXT PAGE ▶

Name _____   Date _____

Unit 5, lesson 4, page 2

3. Which temperature is good swimming weather?
   - Ⓐ 30°F
   - Ⓑ −10°F
   - Ⓒ 82°F
   - Ⓓ 47°F

4. An apple weighs about
   - Ⓔ 5 oz.
   - Ⓕ 6 lbs.
   - Ⓖ 1 T.
   - Ⓗ 3 qt.

5. Two lines that never cross are
   - Ⓐ intersecting.
   - Ⓑ rays.
   - Ⓒ segments.
   - Ⓓ parallel.

6. Which of these figures has a right angle?
   - Ⓔ (hexagon)
   - Ⓕ (triangle)
   - Ⓖ (square)
   - Ⓗ (trapezoid)

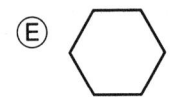

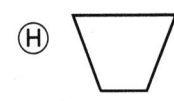

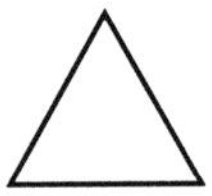

7. Which of these circles has a line showing the diameter?
   - Ⓐ
   - Ⓑ
   - Ⓒ
   - Ⓓ

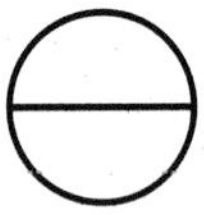

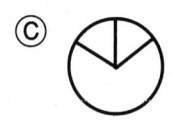

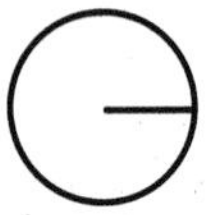

8. What is the perimeter of this five-sided figure?
   - Ⓔ 21 cm 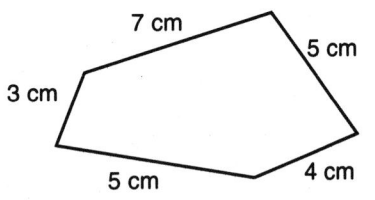
   - Ⓕ 51 cm
   - Ⓖ 28 m
   - Ⓗ 24 cm

   (sides: 7 cm, 5 cm, 3 cm, 5 cm, 4 cm)

9. Which figure shows a line of symmetry?
   - Ⓐ (triangle)
   - Ⓑ (triangle)
   - Ⓒ (hexagon)
   - Ⓓ (parallelogram)

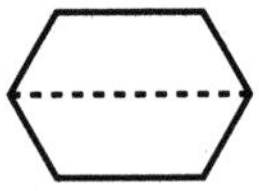

10. If a square is 8 inches on one side, what is its area?
    - Ⓔ 32 square inches
    - Ⓕ 16 square inches
    - Ⓖ 64 square inches
    - Ⓗ 3 square feet

STOP

Your time: _____

Number right: _____

On this lesson I did _____ because _____ .

Name _____ Date _____

PRACTICE TEST 5

Practice Test Answer Sheet, p. 96

Part 1

Directions: For questions 1–9, choose the correct answer to each of the questions below. Choose *E. none* if the correct answer is not given. Record your answer on the answer sheet.

Sample: What is the missing number in this number series?

70, 65, 60, ___ , 50, 45

A 40
B 75
C 59
D 49
E none

Answer: The correct answer is *E. none*. The missing number is 55.

---

1. Which group of numbers is in order from largest to smallest?
   A 7, 9, 11, 15, 19
   B 23, 27, 15, 18, 9
   C 42, 39, 35, 31, 29
   D 29, 31, 35, 39, 42
   E none

2. Which of these numbers is an odd number?
   A 327
   B 248
   C 436
   D 150
   E none

3. Which of these numbers is the same as six thousand fifteen?
   A 6,150
   B 6,105
   C 6,510
   D 6,015
   E none

4. Which number makes both number sentences true?

   4 x ___ = 20   15 + ___ = 20

   A 16
   B 5
   C 6
   D 9
   E none

GO ON TO NEXT PAGE

© Steck-Vaughn Company   79   Test Taking 3, SV 6973-8

Name _____   Date _____

5. Which number is 213 rounded to the nearest ten?

   A 220
   B 215
   C 210
   D 200
   E none

6. Which of these sentences is correct?

   A 4,273 > 5,001
   B 7 > 9
   C 827 < 789
   D 1,203 < 1,103
   E none

7. Which of these numbers has a 6 in the tens place?

   A 6,623
   B 4,306
   C 3,650
   D 5,064
   E none

8. Which clock shows 6:45?

   A
   B
   C
   D
   E none

9. Which of these is the Roman numeral for 36?

   A XXXVI
   B XXXIV
   C XVIXX
   D IVXXX
   E none

Directions: For numbers 10–11, choose the operation that makes the following sentences true.

10. 7 __ 9 = 25 – 9

    A +
    B –
    C ×
    D ÷
    E none

11. 18 + 2 = 10 __ 2

    A +
    B –
    C ×
    D ÷
    E none

GO ON TO NEXT PAGE

Name _____   Date _____

Part 2

Directions: For questions 12–19, choose the correct answer. Choose *E. none* if the correct answer is <u>not given</u>. Record your answer on the answer sheet.

---

12. 73 + 79 =
    - A 142
    - B 153
    - C 152
    - D 1,412
    - E none

13. 93 − 57 =
    - A 36
    - B 46
    - C 54
    - D 150
    - E none

14. 8 x 4 =
    - A 24
    - B 32
    - C 40
    - D 12
    - E none

15. 647
    − 359
    - A 287
    - B 996
    - C 312
    - D 298
    - E none

16. 8,673
    1,519
    + 454
    - A 9,646
    - B 9,546
    - C 10,646
    - D 10,466
    - E none

17. 43
    x 3
    - A 1,209
    - B 129
    - C 79
    - D 46
    - E none

18. 8 ÷ 8 =
    - A 0
    - B 1
    - C 16
    - D 64
    - E none

19. 6)̄54
    - A 8 R5
    - B 9 R1
    - C 9
    - D 8
    - E none

GO ON TO NEXT PAGE

Name _____ Date _____

Part 3

Directions: For questions 20–25, choose the correct answer. Choose *E. none* if the correct answer is <u>not given</u>. Record your answer on the answer sheet.

---

20. Which fraction tells how many dots are shaded?

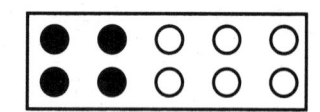

●●○○○
●●○○○

A $\frac{3}{8}$ C $\frac{4}{10}$ E none

B $\frac{4}{4}$ D $\frac{6}{10}$

21. Which is the lowest term of the fraction $\frac{6}{15}$?

A $\frac{2}{5}$ C $\frac{1}{5}$ E none

B $\frac{3}{5}$ D $\frac{3}{10}$

22. $\frac{9}{14}$
   $+ \frac{4}{14}$

A $\frac{5}{0}$ C $\frac{13}{28}$ E none

B $\frac{14}{13}$ D $\frac{5}{14}$

23. Which is the decimal numeral for one and six tenths?

A 1.06 C 10.6 E none
B 0.16 D 1.6

24. 1.2 − 0.6 =

A 1.8 C 0.06 E none
B 1.06 D 1.08

25. $ 0.77
    $+ $ 0.48

A $1.25 C $0.31 E none
B $0.29 D $1.29

GO ON TO NEXT PAGE

Name _____   Date _____

Part 4

Directions: For questions 26–31, choose the correct answer. Choose *E. none* if the correct answer is <u>not given</u>. Record your answer on the answer sheet.

---

26. Which is a reasonable estimate for the height of a 10-year-old child?

  A 4 yd   C 4 ft   E none
  B 7 yd   D 21 in

27. Which temperature means the weather is very cold?

  A 65°F   C 38°F   E none
  B 10°F   D 79°F

28. How much time has passed between the starting and ending times on the clocks?

  START   END

  A 3 hours
  B 2 hours 35 minutes
  C 1 hour 30 minutes
  D 2 hours
  E none

29. What is the perimeter of a square that measures 6 m by 6 m?

  A 24 m   C 12 m   E none
  B 20 m   D 36 m

30. Which number tells how many angles there are in the kite?

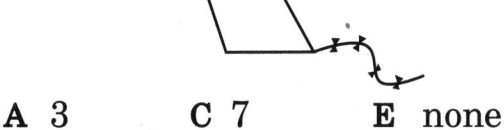

  A 3   C 7   E none
  B 6   D 4

31. Which of the following is a cylinder?

  A   D

  B   E none

  C

STOP

Suggested Time Limit: 33 minutes   Your time: _____

Check your work if you have time. Wait for instructions from your teacher.

Name _____ Date _____

UNIT VI: MATH PROBLEM SOLVING

Lesson 1: Reviewing problem solving strategies
Part one

DIRECTIONS ▶ Darken the circle for the best answer to the strategy question. Darken the circle for *E. none* if the correct answer is <u>not given</u>.

STRATEGY TIPS
1. Look for the pattern strategy.
2. Some problems can be solved by finding a pattern.
3. Find the rule that makes and completes the pattern, then solve the problem.

Sample:
Look for the pattern in the following group of numbers.

65   60   55   50

The pattern is:

Ⓐ add 5   Ⓓ subtract 5
Ⓑ subtract 10   Ⓔ none
Ⓒ add 10

ANSWER
The correct answer is
D. *subtract 5*. Each number has had 5 subtracted from it.

NOW TRY THESE

1. Look for the pattern in the following group of numbers.

   188   288   388   488   588

   Ⓐ subtract 10   Ⓓ add 100
   Ⓑ add 10   Ⓔ none
   Ⓒ multiply by 10

2. Which shape goes next in the pattern?

   ○ △ □ ○ △ □ ○

   Ⓐ □   Ⓓ △
   Ⓑ ○   Ⓔ none
   Ⓒ ▭

GO ON TO NEXT PAGE ▶

© Steck-Vaughn Company   84   Test Taking 3, SV 6973-8

Name _____   Date _____

Lesson 1: Reviewing problem solving strategies Part two

DIRECTIONS ▶ Darken the circle for the best answer to the strategy question. Darken the circle for *E. none* if the correct answer is not given.

STRATEGY TIPS
1. Use a drawing strategy.
2. Sometimes drawing a picture helps to solve a problem.

Sample:

Ms. Cart divided a pizza for 4 people to share equally. Which drawing shows how she divided the pizza?

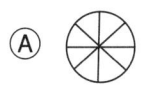

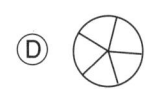

Ⓐ   Ⓓ
Ⓑ   Ⓔ none
Ⓒ

ANSWER
The correct answer is *B*. This pizza is divided in 4 equal slices.

NOW TRY THESE

3. Betty has 6 cookies. She and 2 of her friends will share these cookies equally. Which drawing shows how many cookies each one will get?

   Ⓐ 
   Ⓑ 
   Ⓒ 
   Ⓓ 
   Ⓔ none

4. Selena and her brother are washing windows. If they each wash an equal part of one window, which drawing shows what Selena washes?

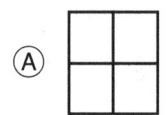

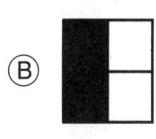

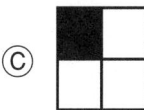

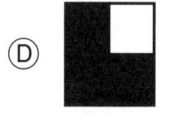

   Ⓐ   Ⓓ
   Ⓑ   Ⓔ none
   Ⓒ

GO ON TO NEXT PAGE ▶

© Steck-Vaughn Company   85   Test Taking 3, SV 6973-8

Name _____   Date _____

Lesson 1: Reviewing problem solving strategies
Part three

DIRECTIONS ▶ Darken the circle for the best answer to the strategy question. Darken the circle for *E. none* if the correct answer is not given.

STRATEGY TIPS
1. Use a list strategy.
2. Making a list can help you organize facts in a problem.

Sample:

Laura is going on a trip. She will take a red shirt, a white shirt, blue jeans, and black shorts. She made a list to see how many different outfits she could make:

Shirts	Pants	Outfits
red	blue jeans	red-blue
white	black shorts	red-black
		white-blue
		white-black

Which number shows how many outfits Laura can make?
Ⓐ 8   Ⓓ 4
Ⓑ 7   Ⓔ none
Ⓒ 6

ANSWER
The correct answer is *D. 4*. From Laura's list you can see she has 4 outfits.

NOW TRY THESE

5. Each day Jason chooses 1 drink and 1 food item to eat for a snack. Today his food choices are pretzels, cookies, or yogurt. His drink choices are fruit juice or milk. Which number shows how many different snacks Jason could have today?

   Ⓐ 3   Ⓓ 8
   Ⓑ 5   Ⓔ none
   Ⓒ 6

6. Keisha wants to make a picture. She can use chalk, paint, or crayons. She may make her picture on yellow paper, white paper, or cardboard. How many different ways can she make a picture?

   Ⓐ 6   Ⓓ 9
   Ⓑ 5   Ⓔ none
   Ⓒ 8

GO ON TO NEXT PAGE ▶

Name _____ Date _____

Lesson 1: Reviewing problem solving strategies
Part four

DIRECTIONS ▶ Darken the circle for the best answer to the strategy question. Darken the circle for *E. none* if the correct answer is <u>not given</u>.

STRATEGY TIPS

1. Use an estimation strategy.
2. Sometimes you do not need an exact answer to solve a problem.
3. The word *about* means you don't need an exact answer.
4. Round each number to the same place, then solve the problem.
5. Read each problem carefully to see which operation to use.

Sample:

Mai Ling's old bookcase held 48 books. Her new bookcase holds 92 books. *About* how many more books does the new bookcase hold than the old bookcase?

Ⓐ 140   Ⓓ 35
Ⓑ 92   Ⓔ none
Ⓒ 40

ANSWER

The correct answer is *C. 40*. Round 48 to 50, and 92 to 90. Subtract the rounded numbers to find that the new bookcase holds *about* 40 more books.

NOW TRY THESE

7. Inez has to fold 202 napkins for the school banquet. She has already folded 87 napkins. *About* how many more napkins does she have to fold?

   Ⓐ 10   Ⓓ 90
   Ⓑ 200   Ⓔ none
   Ⓒ 110

8. Tina bought gumdrops for $1.29 and licorice for $1.12. *About* how much did she spend altogether?

   Ⓐ $3.41   Ⓓ $2.00
   Ⓑ $2.40   Ⓔ none
   Ⓒ $1.40

GO ON TO NEXT PAGE

Name _____ Date _____

Lesson 1: Reviewing problem solving strategies
Part five

DIRECTIONS ▸ Darken the circle for the steps you would use to find the best answer to the strategy question. Darken the circle for *E. none* if the correct answer is not given.

STRATEGY TIPS
1. Use a two-step strategy.
2. Sometimes you need to do more than one step to solve a problem.
3. Read the problem carefully to decide what you need to do.

Sample:

LaShonda made 4 dozen muffins for the bake sale. She also made 36 oatmeal cookies.

How many more muffins than cookies did she make?

Ⓐ 4 x 12, 48 - 36
Ⓑ 4 x 12, 48 + 36
Ⓒ 4 + 12, 45 - 36
Ⓓ 4 x 12, 45 - 36
Ⓔ none

ANSWER

The correct answer is A. *4x12, 48-36*. To find how many muffins are in 4 dozen, multiply. Then subtract to find how many more muffins than cookies she made.

NOW TRY THESE

9. Pedro practiced the piano for 30 minutes on Monday. On Wednesday he practiced 3 times as long as he did on Monday.

   How much time did he practice altogether?

   Ⓐ 30 x 3, 90 + 1
   Ⓑ 30 x 3, 33 + 60
   Ⓒ 30 x 3, 90 + 30
   Ⓓ 30 + 1, 31 x 3
   Ⓔ none

10. Marco bought paper and ribbon. He paid $3.00 for the ribbon and $4.75 for the paper. He got $2.25 in change. How much money did Marco give the clerk?

    Ⓐ $3.00 + $4.75, $7.75 - $2.25
    Ⓑ $3.00 + $4.75, $7.75 + $2.25
    Ⓒ $3.00 - $4.75, $7.75 - $2.25
    Ⓓ $3.00 - $4.75, $7.75 + $2.25
    Ⓔ none

GO ON TO NEXT PAGE ▸

© Steck-Vaughn Company   Test Taking 3, SV 6973-8

Name _____ Date _____

Lesson 1: Reviewing problem solving strategies
Part six

DIRECTIONS ▶ Darken the circle for the best answer to the strategy question. Darken the circle for *E. none* if the correct answer is not given.

STRATEGY TIPS

1. Use an extra information strategy.
2. Some problems have extra facts that you do not need to know to solve the problem. Crossing out these facts can help you solve the problem more quickly.

Sample:

There are 3 birds' nests in the tree. There are 5 eggs in the robin's nest. 2 robin eggs have already hatched. How many eggs are not yet hatched?

Which is the extra fact in this problem?

Ⓐ There are 5 eggs.
Ⓑ There are 3 nests.
Ⓒ 2 eggs have hatched.
Ⓓ The mother robin is sitting on the other eggs.
Ⓔ none

ANSWER

The correct answer is *B. There are 3 nests*. You can solve the problem without this fact.

NOW TRY THESE

11. Kim swims 15 laps in the pool every day. In this pool, 10 laps equal 1 mile. On Tuesday she swims 12 extra laps. How many laps did she swim?

    Which is the extra fact?

    Ⓐ Kim swims 15 laps.
    Ⓑ She swims 12 extra laps.
    Ⓒ 10 laps equal 1 mile.
    Ⓓ Kim swims laps every day.
    Ⓔ none

12. Rosa has an orange for breakfast. Then she eats an apple and a pear at lunch. She doesn't like fuzzy peaches. How many pieces of fruit does Rosa eat? Which is the extra fact in this problem?

    Ⓐ Rosa has an orange for breakfast.
    Ⓑ She eats a pear at lunch.
    Ⓒ She eats an apple at lunch.
    Ⓓ She doesn't like peaches.
    Ⓔ none

Name _____   Date _____

PRACTICE TEST 6

Practice Test Answer Sheet, p. 96

Directions: For questions 1–14, choose the strategy to solve the problem. Darken the circle for *E. none* if the correct answer is <u>not given</u>. Record your answer on the answer sheet.

Sample:
Marty is looking for his friend's house. His friend lives at 125 Main Street. Some of the numbers on the street are 123, 127, and 129. What strategy will Marty use to find his friend's house?

A make a list
B look for the pattern
C estimation
D make a drawing
E none

Answer: The correct answer is *B. look for the pattern.* The pattern shows that Marty's friend's house is between 123 and 127.

---

1. Ramie wants to know how many meals she can make with the food in her kitchen cupboard.

   A two-step
   B extra information
   C make a list
   D look for the pattern
   E none

2. Elin's hen lays 3 eggs a day. How many eggs will her hen lay in 6 days?

   A make a drawing
   B look for a pattern
   C make a list
   D extra information
   E none

GO ON TO NEXT PAGE

© Steck-Vaughn Company   90   Test Taking 3, SV 6973-8

Name _____ Date _____

3. Sheo is older than Jay. Sally is younger than Jay. Maria's age is between Sally's and Sheo's. Who is the youngest?

    A estimation
    B make a drawing
    C look for a pattern
    D extra information
    E none

4. Gino's mother makes 24 cupcakes for a party. Gino and 5 friends eat 3 cupcakes each. How many cupcakes are left?

    A extra information
    B two-step
    C make a list
    D look for a pattern
    E none

5. There are 125 villages in a county. The next county has 93 villages. *About* how many more villages are in the first county?

    A two-step
    B make a list
    C make a drawing
    D estimation
    E none

6. Ms. Wang makes a chocolate cake for her family of 6. She cuts the cake into 12 slices. How many slices can each person have?

    A make a drawing
    B estimation
    C two-step
    D extra information
    E none

7. Roberto has an orange cat and a white cat. He has black, brown, and white collars for his cats. How many different ways can he use the collars for his cats?

    A make a drawing
    B estimation
    C two-step
    D make a list
    E none

8. The bicycle shop has 7 red bikes and 12 blue bikes. There are baskets on the handlebars of 5 red bikes. How many bikes are there in all?

    A estimation
    B two-step
    C extra information
    D make a list
    E none

GO ON TO NEXT PAGE

Name _____   Date _____

9. Dorrie spends $10 for tennis balls, $45 for tennis shoes, and $12 for a t-shirt. How much more did she spend on tennis shoes than on a t-shirt?

   A look for a pattern
   B extra information
   C make a list
   D estimation
   E none

10. Vince is selling tickets to a school play. He started with 128 tickets. He has 72 tickets left. *About* how many did he sell?

    A make a list
    B make a drawing
    C estimation
    D extra information
    E none

11. Avram, Monica, and Jan ride the school bus. Avram rides 3 miles more than Monica. Monica rides half as far as Jan. Jan rides 12 miles. How far does Avram ride?

    A extra information
    B make a list
    C look for a pattern
    D two-step
    E none

12. Jenna's dog has had 3 litters of puppies. The first 2 litters had 4 puppies each. The last litter had 6 puppies. How many puppies has Jenna's dog had?

    A estimation
    B make a drawing
    C look for a pattern
    D extra information
    E none

13. Samir is Runner C in a marathon. Runner A is number 20, Runner B is number 16, and Runner D is number 8. What is Samir's number?

    A look for a pattern
    B extra information
    C make a list
    D two-step
    E none

14. Zoe has 5 mystery books. She has twice as many books about horses. How many books does she have altogether?

    A extra information
    B two-step
    C estimation
    D make a list
    E none

Suggested Time Limit: 20 minutes   Your time: _____

Check your work if you have time. Wait for instructions from your teacher.

TEST TAKING: GRADE 3
ANSWER KEY

Unit I: Word Analysis
Lesson 1, p.8
1. D
2. E
3. C
4. F
5. D
6. G

Lesson 2, pp. 9-11
1. C
2. H
3. A
4. G
5. B
6. H
7. C
8. F
9. A
10. G
11. D
12. E
13. D
14. G
15. D
16. H
17. A
18. G

Lesson 3, pp. 12-13
1. C
2. E
3. D
4. G
5. A
6. F
7. C
8. F
9. C
10. E
11. D
12. F

Practice Test 1, pp.14-16
1. A
2. F
3. D
4. E
5. A
6. F
7. C
8. G
9. A
10. H
11. C
12. E
13. A
14. G
15. A
16. H
17. B
18. G
19. D
20. E
21. D
22. E

Unit II: Vocabulary
Lesson 1, pp. 17-18
1. D
2. G
3. A
4. F
5. B
6. F
7. B
8. H
9. D
10. E
11. B
12. G
13. B
14. G

Lesson 2, pp. 19-20
1. B
2. H
3. C
4. E
5. D
6. F
7. C
8. H
9. B
10. G
11. D
12. G

Lesson 3, pp. 21-22
1. B
2. E
3. C
4. G
5. A
6. F
7. A
8. G
9. A
10. G
11. D
12. G
13. B
14. G
15. C
16. H
17. B
18. E

Lesson 4, pp. 23-24
1. C
2. F
3. D
4. F
5. A
6. E
7. A
8. G
9. D
10. F
11. C
12. H

Lesson 5, pp. 25-28
1. B
2. H
3. A
4. H
5. C
6. F
7. D
8. F
9. C
10. H
11. A
12. F
13. B
14. H
15. B
16. G
17. C
18. E
19. B
20. G
21. D
22. E
23. B
24. E
25. A
26. F
27. C
28. H
29. C
30. E

Practice Test 2, pp. 29-34
1. C
2. F
3. D
4. E
5. C
6. G
7. C
8. H
9. B
10. G
11. D
12. F
13. D
14. G
15. A
16. G
17. A
18. G
19. B
20. H
21. B
22. H
23. A
24. H
25. C
26. F
27. C
28. H
29. C
30. E
31. B
32. G
33. B
34. E

Unit III: Spelling and Language
Lesson 1, pp. 35-36
1. D
2. G
3. B
4. E
5. D
6. F
7. C
8. F
9. B
10. H
11. D
12. E

Lesson 2, pp. 37-38
1. A
2. C
3. B
4. E
5. D
6. D
7. B
8. B
9. C
10. A

Lesson 3, pp. 39-40
1. D
2. C
3. A
4. E
5. E
6. E
7. D
8. C
9. A
10. E
11. B
12. B
13. C
14. E

Lesson 4, pp. 41-43
1. D
2. E
3. B
4. G
5. A
6. G
7. A
8. H
9. C
10. F
11. C
12. G

TEST TAKING: GRADE 3
ANSWER KEY

Practice Test 3, pp. 44-47
1. A
2. D
3. B
4. A
5. B
6. C
7. D
8. A
9. B
10. C
11. A
12. E
13. B
14. D
15. C
16. A
17. B
18. E
19. D
20. E
21. C
22. D
23. B
24. A

Unit IV: Reading Comprehension
Lesson 1, pp. 48-54
1. C
2. F
3. D
4. F
5. D
6. G
7. B
8. H
9. C
10. G
11. A
12. G
13. A
14. F
15. C
16. G
17. A
18. F
19. A
20. F
21. D

Lesson 2, pp. 55-56
1. A
2. H
3. B
4. H
5. C

Lesson 3, pp. 57-59
1. A
2. G
3. D
4. F
5. A
6. H
7. A
8. E
9. B
10. H

Practice Test 4, pp. 60-65
1. B
2. H
3. B
4. H
5. C
6. E
7. A
8. H
9. C
10. H
11. A
12. H
13. C
14. E
15. B
16. H
17. A
18. F
19. D
20. H

Unit V: Math Practice
Lesson 1, pp. 66-68
1. B
2. C
3. B
4. E
5. B
6. C
7. B
8. A
9. C
10. A
11. B
12. B
13. C
14. A

Lesson 2, pp 69-74
1. C
2. H
3. B
4. E
5. B
6. G
7. B
8. E or G
9. C
10. H
11. B
12. H
13. B
14. E
15. C
16. A
17. B
18. C
19. D
20. B
21. B
22. B
23. C
24. B
25. B
26. B
27. C
28. D
29. C
30. B
31. B
32. B

Lesson 3, pp. 75-76
1. D
2. C
3. A
4. D
5. B
6. E
7. B
8. C
9. C
10. B

Lesson 4, pp. 77-78
1. B
2. G
3. C
4. E
5. D
6. G
7. A
8. H
9. C
10. G

Practice Test 5, pp. 79-83
1. C
2. A
3. D
4. B
5. C
6. E
7. D
8. C
9. A
10. A
11. C
12. C
13. A
14. B
15. E
16. C
17. B
18. B
19. C
20. C
21. A
22. E
23. B
24. E
25. A
26. C
27. B
28. B
29. A
30. D
31. D

Unit VI: Problem Solving
Lesson 1, pp. 84-89
1. D
2. D
3. C
4. B
5. C
6. D
7. C
8. B
9. C
10. B
11. C
12. D

Practice Test 6, pp. 90-92
1. C
2. A
3. B
4. B
5. D
6. A
7. D
8. C
9. B
10. C
11. D
12. B
13. A
14. B

Name _____   Date _____

Practice Test ____ Answer Sheet

1. Ⓐ Ⓑ Ⓒ Ⓓ   21. Ⓐ Ⓑ Ⓒ Ⓓ
2. Ⓔ Ⓕ Ⓖ Ⓗ   22. Ⓔ Ⓕ Ⓖ Ⓗ
3. Ⓐ Ⓑ Ⓒ Ⓓ   23. Ⓐ Ⓑ Ⓒ Ⓓ
4. Ⓔ Ⓕ Ⓖ Ⓗ   24. Ⓔ Ⓕ Ⓖ Ⓗ
5. Ⓐ Ⓑ Ⓒ Ⓓ   25. Ⓐ Ⓑ Ⓒ Ⓓ
6. Ⓔ Ⓕ Ⓖ Ⓗ   26. Ⓔ Ⓕ Ⓖ Ⓗ
7. Ⓐ Ⓑ Ⓒ Ⓓ   27. Ⓐ Ⓑ Ⓒ Ⓓ
8. Ⓔ Ⓕ Ⓖ Ⓗ   28. Ⓔ Ⓕ Ⓖ Ⓗ
9. Ⓐ Ⓑ Ⓒ Ⓓ   29. Ⓐ Ⓑ Ⓒ Ⓓ
10. Ⓔ Ⓕ Ⓖ Ⓗ   30. Ⓔ Ⓕ Ⓖ Ⓗ
11. Ⓐ Ⓑ Ⓒ Ⓓ   31. Ⓐ Ⓑ Ⓒ Ⓓ
12. Ⓔ Ⓕ Ⓖ Ⓗ   32. Ⓔ Ⓕ Ⓖ Ⓗ
13. Ⓐ Ⓑ Ⓒ Ⓓ   33. Ⓐ Ⓑ Ⓒ Ⓓ
14. Ⓔ Ⓕ Ⓖ Ⓗ   34. Ⓔ Ⓕ Ⓖ Ⓗ
15. Ⓐ Ⓑ Ⓒ Ⓓ   35. Ⓐ Ⓑ Ⓒ Ⓓ
16. Ⓔ Ⓕ Ⓖ Ⓗ   36. Ⓔ Ⓕ Ⓖ Ⓗ
17. Ⓐ Ⓑ Ⓒ Ⓓ   37. Ⓐ Ⓑ Ⓒ Ⓓ
18. Ⓔ Ⓕ Ⓖ Ⓗ   38. Ⓔ Ⓕ Ⓖ Ⓗ
19. Ⓐ Ⓑ Ⓒ Ⓓ   39. Ⓐ Ⓑ Ⓒ Ⓓ
20. Ⓔ Ⓕ Ⓖ Ⓗ   40. Ⓔ Ⓕ Ⓖ Ⓗ

© Steck-Vaughn Company   Test Taking 3, SV 6973-8

Name _____   Date _____

Practice Test ____ Answer Sheet

1. Ⓐ Ⓑ Ⓒ Ⓓ Ⓔ   21. Ⓐ Ⓑ Ⓒ Ⓓ Ⓔ
2. Ⓐ Ⓑ Ⓒ Ⓓ Ⓔ   22. Ⓐ Ⓑ Ⓒ Ⓓ Ⓔ
3. Ⓐ Ⓑ Ⓒ Ⓓ Ⓔ   23. Ⓐ Ⓑ Ⓒ Ⓓ Ⓔ
4. Ⓐ Ⓑ Ⓒ Ⓓ Ⓔ   24. Ⓐ Ⓑ Ⓒ Ⓓ Ⓔ
5. Ⓐ Ⓑ Ⓒ Ⓓ Ⓔ   25. Ⓐ Ⓑ Ⓒ Ⓓ Ⓔ
6. Ⓐ Ⓑ Ⓒ Ⓓ Ⓔ   26. Ⓐ Ⓑ Ⓒ Ⓓ Ⓔ
7. Ⓐ Ⓑ Ⓒ Ⓓ Ⓔ   27. Ⓐ Ⓑ Ⓒ Ⓓ Ⓔ
8. Ⓐ Ⓑ Ⓒ Ⓓ Ⓔ   28. Ⓐ Ⓑ Ⓒ Ⓓ Ⓔ
9. Ⓐ Ⓑ Ⓒ Ⓓ Ⓔ   29. Ⓐ Ⓑ Ⓒ Ⓓ Ⓔ
10. Ⓐ Ⓑ Ⓒ Ⓓ Ⓔ   30. Ⓐ Ⓑ Ⓒ Ⓓ Ⓔ
11. Ⓐ Ⓑ Ⓒ Ⓓ Ⓔ   31. Ⓐ Ⓑ Ⓒ Ⓓ Ⓔ
12. Ⓐ Ⓑ Ⓒ Ⓓ Ⓔ   32. Ⓐ Ⓑ Ⓒ Ⓓ Ⓔ
13. Ⓐ Ⓑ Ⓒ Ⓓ Ⓔ   33. Ⓐ Ⓑ Ⓒ Ⓓ Ⓔ
14. Ⓐ Ⓑ Ⓒ Ⓓ Ⓔ   34. Ⓐ Ⓑ Ⓒ Ⓓ Ⓔ
15. Ⓐ Ⓑ Ⓒ Ⓓ Ⓔ   35. Ⓐ Ⓑ Ⓒ Ⓓ Ⓔ
16. Ⓐ Ⓑ Ⓒ Ⓓ Ⓔ   36. Ⓐ Ⓑ Ⓒ Ⓓ Ⓔ
17. Ⓐ Ⓑ Ⓒ Ⓓ Ⓔ   37. Ⓐ Ⓑ Ⓒ Ⓓ Ⓔ
18. Ⓐ Ⓑ Ⓒ Ⓓ Ⓔ   38. Ⓐ Ⓑ Ⓒ Ⓓ Ⓔ
19. Ⓐ Ⓑ Ⓒ Ⓓ Ⓔ   39. Ⓐ Ⓑ Ⓒ Ⓓ Ⓔ
20. Ⓐ Ⓑ Ⓒ Ⓓ Ⓔ   40. Ⓐ Ⓑ Ⓒ Ⓓ Ⓔ

© Steck-Vaughn Company   Test Taking 3, SV 6973-8